THE CALL OF GOD IN JESUS CHRIST FOR HOLINESS AND SOCIAL MORALITY

FIFTEEN TEXTUAL SERMONS ON THE LENT

WITH

'METHODIST PIETY AND SOCIAL MORALITY OR SCRIPTURAL HOLINESS OF METHODISM'

THE CALL OF GOD IN JESUS CHRIST FOR HOLINESS AND SOCIAL MORALITY

FIFTEEN TEXTUAL SERMONS ON THE LENT
WITH
'METHODIST PIETY AND SOCIAL MORALITY OR SCRIPTURAL HOLINESS OF METHODISM'

Daniel D. Rupwate

2021

The Call of God in Jesus Christ for Holiness and Social Morality: Fifteen Textual Sermons on the Lent with 'Methodist Piety and Social Morality or Scriptural Holiness of Methodism' - Published by the Indian Society for Promoting Christian Knowledge (ISPCK), Post Box 1585, Kashmere Gate, Delhi-110006.

ISBN: 978-93-90569-24-3

Laser typeset by

ISPCK, Post Box 1585, 1654, Madarsa Road, Kashmere Gate, Delhi-110006 • *Tel:* 23866323

e-mail: ashish@ispck.org.in • ella@ispck.org.in
website: www.ispck.org.in

Dedication

Rev. Joshua David   and   Mrs Lucy J David
(27/12/1911- 18/08/1995)   (06/11/1920- 19/01/1989)

REV. JOSHUA DAVID AND MRS. LUCY J. DAVID

This book is dedicated to the late Rev. Joshua David (December 27, 1911-August 8, 1995) and his wife the late Mrs. Lucy J. David (November 6, 1920-January 19,1989) for their affection and concerns for my wellbeing.

Rev. Joshua David served the Methodist Church in Southern Asia. After his matriculation, he was admitted in Leonard Theologica College, Jabalpur, Maddhya Pradesh, India. He got a diploma called 'Graduate in Theology (G. Th.) from this theological college. The details of his educational background were not available unfortunately. It was reported that Rev. Joshua David began to serve the Methodist Church in 1941; and he continued his services to the Methodist Church until his death in 1995. This means that he served the church for fifty-four years. This is indeed a long service.

Rev. Joshua David served the Methodist Church in various capacities, such a minister, a District Superintendent, and a manager of high school. The details of his ministry were not available. He was a dedicated minister and efficient manager. It should be noted that the Mecossabagh school in Nagpur was updated to a high school level because of dedication to the work of God.

I was appointed by the Bombay Annual Conference of the Methodist Church in Southern Asia as an assistant minister at Marathi Methodist Church, Nagpur in 1963, for a year, after I completed B. D. from Leonard Theological College, Jabalpur. Rev. Joshua was the minister-in-charge of the Marathi Methodist Church, Nagpur. He was also serving the church as a District Superintendent of the mission district Nagpur.

Rev. Joshua David and his wife Mrs. Lucy J. David cordially welcomed me in their family and provided me an accommodation in their residence; and provided me food. They made me feel that I was a member of their large family. Mrs. Lucy David was very loving and hospitable lady. She was taking care of their nine children. She was very hard working mother, taking care of her large family. I was very fortunate to be a part of their large family.

Rev. Joshua David was a caring a compassionate gentle man. He was well aware of a financial condition of ministers in general. He expressed his concern towards me and gave me an opportunity of serving as a supplied teacher in the Mecossabagh High School Nagpur, in his capacity of the manager of the high school. He was exceptional in caring others' need. I was able to meet my financial obligations by this additional service. I shall never forget his kindness.

Rev. Joshua David and Mrs. Lucy David showed their affection and kindness towards me. I considered them as my second parents. Therefore, I consider my privilege to dedicate this book to them in their loving remembrance and with my sincere gratitude to them.

Daniel D. Rupwate

Contents

Part II
'METHODIST PIETY AND SOCIAL MORALITY OR SCRIPTURAL HOLINESS OF METHODISM'

Acknowledgements

First, this book was edited by late Mr. Harry Harper and Mrs. June Harper, the members of the British Methodist Episcopal Church, at St. Catharines, Ontario. The writer is grateful for their volunteer labour.

The writer is grateful to Rev. Jonah J. David from Thane, Maharashtra State, India, for providing the information of his parents, late Rev. Joshua David and late Mrs. Lucy J. David.

The writer is grateful to his daughter Shelini Rupwate for her technical support in writing the book.

"Quotations in the book are from the Revised Standard Version unless stated otherwise".

Preface

Lenten Season is a very important season in the calendar of the universal Church, because during this season believers are expected to have a closer walk with God in Jesus Christ. Preachers and teachers of the gospel of Jesus Christ are expected to help the believers have a closer walk with God and deepen their understanding about the biblical piety or holiness and social morality.

Alike Christianity, there are world religions namely, Hinduism, Buddhism, Jainism, Sikhism, Taoism, Shintoism, Confucianism, Zoroastrianism, Islam, and Judaism. These religions have different notions of holiness. Believers in Christianity should know how the notion of holiness of Christianity is different from other kinds of holiness, taught by other world religions. Nevertheless, this is not the purpose of this book. The purpose of this book is to know holiness from a Christian point of view.

A pursuit of a biblical holiness was demonstrated by Methodist movement in eighteenth century. The Methodist movement was a reform movement, grounded in Christian piety. Rev. John Wesley was a founder and a scholar of Methodism. He taught Christian piety to the people called Methodist. His thoughts about piety or holiness may help the existing Methodist Churches to go back to the basic teaching of Rev. John Wesley and to re-enforce piety among Methodists.

The book is divided into two parts. The first part of this book is called *"A BIBLICAL HOLINESS: Lenten Fourteen Textual Sermons."* These sermons or essays are intended to deepen understanding about a biblical holiness in general.

The second part has one chapter only. The last chapter of the book bears the title, "Methodist Piety and Social Morality or the Scriptural Holiness of Methodism." This essay was the written for the Canadian Methodist Historical Society in 1994. This essay will help the readers to know a scriptural holiness from a point of Methodism. The essay is gone beyond the Methodist concept of holiness or piety; and it has alluded to the modern writers, dealing with holiness in general. Therefore, the essay would help any Christian believer to know the biblical holiness, irrespective of his or her denominational background.

Daniel D. Rupwate,
Hamilton, Ontario, Canada.

Part I

FIFTEEN TEXTUAL SERMONS ON THE LENT

Chapter 1

'Lovingkindness of God to His People,'
'Divine Lovingkindness to God's Chosen People,'
'A History of God's Forgiveness and Man's Stubbornness,'
'Repeated Manifestation of God's Mercy on the Repentant.'

Scripture

Nehemiah 9:16-31

Genesis 11:31; 15:18-21; 17:3-7

Exodus 1:6-14; 2:15; 3:7-10; 7:14-21; 8:3-6, 16-17,19,

21-22; 9:3, 8-10, 18-25; 10:7, 12-15, 21-22; 11:4-6; 12:40-41; 14:10, 19-20, 24; 16:3, 12-13,35; 17:3, 6; 32:9-10, 11-14, 28, 32

Numbers 11:31; 14:1-4, 14, 17-19, 32-34; 20:8

Judges 3:12-30; 4; 7:1-8:28; 10:7-8; 14-16

I Samuel 7:5-16; 10:1-2; 16:12-13

II Samuel 5:4-5

Ezra 1:1ff.

Nehemiah 2:3-4

Isaiah 40:1; 44:28-45:6

Text: Nehemiah 9:28

A Few Versions of the Text, Nehemiah 9:28

But after they had rest, they again did evil before You. Therefore You left them in the hand of their enemies, So that they had dominion over them; Yet when they turned and cried out You, You heard from heaven; And many times You delivered them, according to Your mercies. *New King James Version*

But after they had rest, they did evil again before thee; therefore leftest thou them in the hand of their enemies, so that they had the dominion over them: yet when they returned, and cried unto thee, thou heardest from heaven; and many times didst thou deliver them according to thy mercies, *The Wesleyan Bible Commentary*

But after they had rest they did evil again before thee; and thou didst abandon them to the hand of their enemies, so that they had dominion over them; yet when they turned and cried to thee thou didst hear from heaven, and many times thou didst deliver them according to thy mercies. *Revised Standard Version*

But as soon as they were at rest, they again did what was evil in your sight. Then you abandoned them to the hand of their enemies so that they ruled over them. And when they cried out to you again, you heard from heaven, and in your compassion you delivered them time after time. *New International Version*

But, when they had a respite, they once more did what was wrong in thine eyes; and thou didst abandon them to their enemies who held them in subjection. But again they cried to thee for help, and many times over thou heardest them from heaven and in thy compassion didst save them. *The New English Bible*

But when all going well, your people turned to sin again, and once more you let their enemies conquer them. Yet whenever your people returned to you and cried to you for help, once more you listened from heaven, and in your wonderful mercy delivered them! *The Living Bible Illustrated*

As soon as they felt some relief, they were again doing what you considered evil. You abandoned them to their enemies, who conquered them. They cried to you again, and you heard them from heaven. You rescued them many times because of your compassion. *God's Word*

Introduction

The churches in the world observe the Lent every year in order to prepare the believers to understand the sufferings of Jesus Christ and to walk in a newness of spiritual life in Him. The believers fast, pray, and meditate on the Holy Scripture every day, during a Lenten season.

An observance of the Lent has become an old tradition. The lent is forty-day fast, extending from Ash Wednesday through Easter eve. Six Sundays are not observed as fast days. The lent began as a commemoration of the forty hours, from the Crucifixion to the Resurrection of Jesus Christ. The period was justified by the facts that Jesus Christ was tested in the wilderness for forty days; and he was fasting during the period (Mt. 4:2). Like Jesus Christ, Moses (Ex. 34:28) and Elijah fasted (I Kg. 19:8) for forty days. The early church fathers, St. Iranaeus (ca. A. D.138-198) and St. Gregory of Nazianzus (ca. A. D. 330-389), had justified so. By the seventh century, the Lenten period became standardized at forty days.[1]

Devout Christians observe the Lent to turn away from sins and toward God. They personally and collectively repent of their sins and ask God for His forgiveness of their sins and for spiritual strength to walk righteously before Him. For this reason, the Lenten season could be called "Cross Bearing or Crucilation, the willingness to bear one's cross in following Christ." This is the message of the lent. Therefore, it is the most demanding of the spiritual seasons of Christian Calender.[2] Lenten Season is mainly featured with a spiritual fasting and repentance.

Introduction of the Text

Repentance is an old theme of the Bible. Repentance means, on one hand, that man realizes his sins of deviating from the teaching of the word of God or breaking the commandments of the LORD God. Man feels a genuine sorrow for his evil deeds and wicked thoughts. He wishes to redesign himself in accordance with the word of God. Repentance implies, on the one hand, that God shows His lovingkindness to man, on the other hand, He forgives man his sins and saves him from the eternal punishment. These spiritual acts of man and of God were repeated in the history of the Jews. Ezra, the high priest and a scribe, told these facts to Jews in his address to them, saying:

> **But after they had rest they did evil again before thee; and thou didst abandon them to the hand of their enemies, so that they had dominion over them; yet when they turned and cried to thee thou didst hear from heaven, and many times thou didst deliver them according to thy mercies. (Nehemiah 9: 28)**

This is the text of our meditation now.

The Context of the Text

In these words of the text, Ezra told the Jews how the LORD God had been dealing with them in His lovingkindness and steadfast love. Ezra was the high priest and a scribe of the Jews in Jerusalem. Ezra and the Governor Nehemiah (ca. 445-433 B. C.) were working together for a common goal, which was to restore the worship of the LORD God. The restoration of the worship of God Yahweh included rebuilding the temple of God and repairing walls around Jerusalem.

Ezra and Nehemiah had also a common political background. Nebuchadrezzar, the emperor of Babylon, (605-562 B. C.) destroyed Jerusalem and the temple of God in 588 B. C. He took Jews captive to Babylon. Ezra and Nehemiah were among the captives. The exiled Jews settled in Babylon; they built synagogues to worship God Yahweh. The Babylonian empire was short-lived. Cyrus (539-530 B. C.), the Persian emperor, defeated the Babylonian empire in 538 B. C. He acted as an instrument of God Yahweh (Is. 44:28-45:6). He allowed Jews to return to Palestine and to restore the temple of God in Jerusalem (Ezra 1:1ff. cf. Is. 40:1). Haggai and Zechariah, the prophets, returned to Jerusalem; and rebuilt the temple of God. But the walls of Jerusalem were left to be repaired.

After Cyrus, Artaxerxes I (465-424 B. C.) became an emperor of Persia. He continued the liberal policy of the emperor Cyrus toward Jews. Ezra returned to Jerusalem in 458 B. C., in the seventh year of the rule of Artaxerxes I. Nehemiah joined Ezra in 445 B. C. Nehemiah was rich; he was holding an influential position of a cupbearer to the emperor Artaxerxes I. He received a gloomy report of the situation at Jerusalem. When he gave a cup to the emperor, the emperor noticed that Nehemiah was sad. When the king asked the reason of his sadness, Nehemiah explained the king the reason of his sadness (Neh. 2:3-4). The king granted him permission to repair the walls of Jerusalem; and also appointed Nehemiah as the governor of Judah (445-433 B. C.).

Nehemiah went to Jerusalem in 445 B. C. He told his intention to the Jews that he would repair or rebuild the walls of Jerusalem. The people liked his proposal; and they worked with him. They rebuilt the walls of Jerusalem within six months.

After rebuilding the walls of Jerusalem, the leaders of the people and the people started a work of religious revival, in the seventh month. Ezra, the high priest, and Nehemiah, the governor, and other leaders decided to hold an assembly on the twenty-fourth day; it was a day of repentance. People were fasting, wearing sack cloth, and putting earth upon their heads, on that day. In the assembly, Ezra reviewed a history of Israel from the period of the call of God to Abraham to the period of the return of the exiles to Palestine. He told the people, how God had been dealing with them and how the people were acting against the will of the LORD God, in the following words:

> But after they had rest they did evil again before thee; and thou didst abandon them to the hand of their enemies, so that they had dominion over them; yet when they turned and cried to thee thou didst hear

from heaven, and many times thou didst deliver them according to thy mercies. (Neh. 9:28)

This is the text, within its historical background.

An Analysis of the Text

The text has four ideas.

> (A) The people of Israel again did evil in the sight of God, after they had rest from afflictions, imposed by their enemies.

> (B) God abandoned the people of Israel because they committed sins against Him; they were subjected to their enemies.

> (C) When the people of Israel cried to God to deliver them from their enemies, God heard their cry.

(D) God delivered them many times according to His mercy and lovingkindness.

An Exposition of the Ideas of the Text

These ideas of the text should not be explained separately because they talk about the sequence of the redemptive history of Israel, which was repeated often. The sequence of the events in the redemptive history is as follows: The people of Israel sinned against God; God abandoned His people, He allowed the enemies of Israel to subject them to afflictions; the people of Israel repented of their sins and they cried to God to deliver them from the affliction; the LORD God heard their cry and delivered them many times, according to His mercy and lovingkindness.

In order to explain the sequence of the events in the redemptive history, we have to mention some of these events. This should be a way or technique to explain the textual ideas.

(1) Ezra began to review a history of Israel from the period of the call of God to Abraham. He stated that God chose Abram and brought him from Ur of the Chaldeans (Gen. 11:31) to the promised land. God found Abram faithful; and He changed his name from Abram

to Abraham (Gen. 17: 3-7). He made a covenant with Abraham that He would give the land of the Canaanites, the Hittites, the Amorites, the Perizzites, the Jebusites, and the Girgashites, to the descendants of Abraham (Gen. 15:18-21). God fulfilled His promise when the Hebrews settled in the promised land.

Joseph and his brothers settled in Egypt; and they were greatly multiplied. After the death of Joseph, there was a new king of Egypt, Seti I (1319-1301 B. C.); he did not know about Joseph (Ex. 1:8). When he saw the people of Israel were more than Egyptians, he devised a plan to control Israelites. He made Israelites as slaves, working for Egyptians for nothing (Ex.1: 6-14). Israelites were in slavery for many generation until God raised Moses to liberate them.

(2) Ezra then referred to the period from liberating Hebrews from Egyptian bondage to their journey through the wilderness. During this period, God was showing His lovingkindness to the Hebrews and yet they were not obedient to Him. This became a typical pattern of behaviour of the Hebrews.

Ezra mentioned some of the events which took place during the period. God heard the affliction of Hebrews. God spared the life of Moses in order to raise him to be a leader of Hebrews. Moses fled to Midian because he was afraid of being tried by Pharaoh, because he killed an Egyptian (Ex. 2:15). God appeared to Moses in the burning bush and He told to Moses the purpose of His appearing to him, in the following words:

> I have seen the afflictions of my people who are in Egypt, and I have heard their cry because of their taskmasters; I know their sufferings, and I have come down to deliver them out of the hand of the Egyptians, and bring them up out of that land to a good and broad land, a land flowing with milk and honey, to the place of the Canaanites, the Hittites, the Amorites, the Perizzites, the Hivites, and the Jebusites. And now, behold, the cry of the people of Israel has come to me, and I have seen the oppression with which the Egyptians oppress them. Come, I will send you to Pharaoh that you may bring forth my people, the sons of Israel, out of Egypt. (Ex. 3:7-10)

God appointed Moses to be the liberator of the people of Israel from the Egyptian bondage. Moses was able to perform ten mighty miracles or plagues (Ex. 7:14-21; 8:3-6, 16-17, 21-22; 9:3, 8-10, 18-25; 10:12-15, 21-22; 11:4-6) to convince the Egyptians and their king Ramses II (1301-1234 B. C.) that God was behind the act of liberation of Israel (Ex.8:19; 10:7). The exodus of Hebrews from Egypt took place after 1300 B. C.[3] God ended the slavery of Israel which lasted for four hundred and thirty years (Ex.12: 40-41).

Ezra mentioned the divine act of dividing the Red Sea and giving a safe passage to the people of Israel through the sea, when the people cried to the LORD God (Ex. 14:10). When the people of Israel were passing through the Red Sea and the army of Egyptians was behind them, the pillar of the LORD God stood between the people of Israel and the army of Egyptians (Ex. 14:19-20). The pillar of the LORD God is also called as the pillar of fire and cloud (Ex. 14:24).

The pillar of the LORD God was leading the people of Israel through the wilderness; it became the pillar of cloud by day and pillar of fire by night (Num. 14:14). While the pillar of the LORD God was leading the people of Israel through the wilderness, the people murmured against the LORD God many times. When they had no food, they murmured against Moses and Aaron in the wilderness, saying:

> Would that we had died by the hand of the LORD in the land of Egypt, when we sat by the fleshpots and ate bread to the full; for you have brought us out into this wilderness to kill this whole assembly with hunger. (Ex. 16:3)

In the evening quails came up and covered the camp (Num.11:31) and in the morning dew lay round about the camp (Ex.16:13). In the morning God provided food and in the evening, flesh, to the people (Ex. 16:12). God supplied the manna to the people for forty years (Ex. 16:35). He did not withhold manna, when the people murmured against God and His servants.

When the people camped at Rephidim, there was no water to drink. Therefore, the people murmured against Moses, saying, "Why did you bring us out of Egypt, to kill us and our children and our cattle with thirst?" (Ex. 17:3) God asked Moses to strike on the rock at Horeb and water came out of it and the people drank the water (Ex. 17:6; Num. 20:8).

When the people reached the mount Sinai, God gave them ten commandments and other laws through Moses (Ex. 19-31). As Moses was delayed to come down from the mountain, the people asked Aaron to make gods for them. People brought gold to Aaron; he melted it; and a golden calf came out of it. They worshipped the molten calf as their god; therefore, the LORD God was displeased with them; and they made Him very angry (Ex. 32:10). However, Moses pleaded for the people; and God changed His mind from destroying the people of Israel (Ex. 32:11-14). God saved the people for the sake of His servants, Abraham, Isaac, and Jacob, and for keeping His promise to give the promised land as their inheritance (Ex. 32:13-14).

The people of Israel were stiff-necked people in the sight of the LORD God (Ex. 32:9). They murmured against the LORD God and His servants, Moses and Aaron, many times. God asked Moses to send twelve tribal leaders to spy the promised land. They spied the land for forty days. They brought good and bad reports. The good report was that the land was with milk and honey; but the bad report was that the inhabitants of the land were stronger than the people of Israel (Ex. 13:28, 32). The people of Israel were sore afraid.

> They murmured against Moses and Aaron, saying:Would that we had died in the land of Egypt! Or would that we had died in this wilderness! Why does the LORD bring us into this land, to fall by the sword? Our wives and our little ones will become a prey; would it not be better for us to go back to Egypt? (Num. 14:2-3)

They said to one another to choose a captain and to go back to Egypt (Num. 14:4). Aaron and Caleb encouraged the people to trust in the LORD God, but the people threw stones at them. The LORD God was angry at the people, wishing to destroy them with pestilence. Moses pleaded to the LORD God, saying:

> And now, I pray thee, let the power of the LORD be great as thou hast promised, saying, ' The LORD is slow to anger, and abounding in steadfast love, forgiving iniquity and transgression, but he will by no means clear them guilty, visiting the iniquity of fathers upon children, upon the third and fourth generation.' Pardon the iniquity of this people, I pray thee, according to the greatness of thy steadfast love and according as thou hast forgiven this people, from Egypt even until now. (Num. 14:17-19)

The people of Israel wandered in the wilderness for forty years because of their faithlessness; and all those who disobeyed God died in the wilderness (Num. 14:32-34). During forty years, God showed His steadfast love to the people of Israel; the pillar of God did not depart from them; He provided manna and water to the rebellious people.

(3) Ezra then referred to the period of when the people of Israel began to settle in the promised land. During this period, people rebelled against the LORD God; they killed His prophets; God gave them in the hand of their enemies. When they cried to the LORD God, God sent saviours to save them.

Joshua defeated the enemies of Israel; he took possession of the promised land; he divided the land among the eleven tribes (Jos.13-19). The people served the LORD God during the time of Joshua and the elders who outlived him. But the religious situation changed after them; the people began to worship Baals and Ashtaroth; therefore the wrath of the LORD God kindled against them and He delivered them to their enemies to be plundered (Jud. 2:6-15). The LORD God heard the cries of Israel and He took pity on them. Then the LORD raised judges to save them from their enemies. The people served the LORD during the time of judges. But whenever judges died, they turned back and behaved worse than their fathers; they did not change their way of stubbornness (Jud. 2:18-19). Let us refer to a few events.

(a) When the people of Israel began to serve Baal and Ashtaroth, the anger of the LORD kindled against them. He handed them into the hand of Cushan-rishathaim, the king of Mesopotamia, for eight years. People of Israel cried to the LORD and God raised Othniel a judge, who defeated the oppressing king of Mesopotamia. The people of Israel had rest for forty years (Jud.3:7-11).

(b) The people of Israel sinned against the LORD; He put them in the hand of Eglon, the king of Moab for eighteen years. Then the people of Israel cried to the LORD, He raised Ehud as a judge. Ehud killed Eglon. He sounded the trumpet in the hill country of Ephraim; people of Israel followed him; and they killed all strong Moabites. Then the people of Israel had rest for eighty years (Jud. 3:12-30).

(c) After the death of Ehud, the people of Israel sinned against the LORD. God handed them into the hand of Jabin, the king of Canaan. His commander was Sisera. Prophetess Deborah was judging the people of Israel. She encouraged Barak to go against Sisera. Sisera was killed by a woman; and she presented the dead body of Barak. The people of Israel became stronger and stronger; and they destroyed Jabin, king of Canaan. (Jud. 4).

(d) The people of Israel sinned against the LORD; He delivered them into the hands of Midianites and Amalekites; they used to destroy the crop and animals of Israel, about seven years. The people cried to the LORD. God raised Gideon to liberate the people of Israel from oppression. Gideon killed the kings of Midianites and Amalekites and their army. There was rest forty years in the days of Gideon (Jud. 7:1-8:28).

(e) After the death of Gideon, the people of Israel sinned against the LORD by worshipping gods of Sidon, of Moab, of Ammorites, and of the Philistines. God delivered them into the hands of the Philistines; and they oppressed them for eighteen years (Jud. 10:7-8). God raised Jephtah to be a judge; after him, there were others judges. God raised Samson to deliver the people of Israel from the Philistines (Jud. 14-16). God raised Samuel to be a priest, a prophet, and a judge of the people of Israel in order to liberate them from the Philistines (I Sam. 7:5-16). Samuel anointed Saul to be a king of Israel (1044-1004 B. C.) and to fight against the Philistines (I Sam. 10:1-2). When Saul disobeyed God, God asked Samuel to anoint David as a king of Israel (I Sam. 16:12-13).

David (1002-962 B. C.) unified the twelve tribes of Israel and established a kingdom (II Sam. 5:4-5).

(4) Ezra mentioned the period from the time of the kings of Assyria to his present day, when the princes, priests, prophets and all the people of Israel suffered hardship (Neh. 9:32-34).

After king Solomon (962-922 B. C.), the kingdom of the people of Israel was divided into two kingdoms- Southern Kingdom or the Kingdom of Judah, and Northern Kingdom or the Kingdom of Israel. Majority of those kings sinned against the LORD God by worshipping other gods; the wrath of God kindled against them; and He punished the people of Israel through foreign rulers.

Ezra referred to the kings of Assyria in his address to the people, who returned from Babylon to Jerusalem. Hoshea was the king of Israel (732-724 B. C.); he ruled nine years. He sinned against the LORD God. Shalmaneser V (727-722 B. C.) was the emperor of Assyria. He made war against Hoshea; and made him to pay tribute every year. When Hoshea stopped paying tribute to Shalmaneser V, he invaded Israel and besieged Samaria in 722 B. C. In the third year of besiege, the emperor of Assyria, probably Sargon II (722-705 B. C.), the successor of Shalmaneser V, and in the last year of Hoshea, captured Samaria in 721 B. C.; he took the Israelites as prisoners and settled them in the city of Halah, River Habor, and in the cities of Media (II Kg. 17:5).

The main reason of the fall of the Northern Kingdom was that the people worshipped other gods and disobeyed the LORD's command not to worship idols. (II Kg. 17:8-12; Ezek. 39:23-24) In the fourteenth year of King Hezekiah (715-687 B. C.), Sennacherib king of Assyria (705-681 B. C.), in 701 B. C. came up against all fortified cities of Judah and took them. King Hezekiah asked King Sennacherib to withdraw from him; and paid King Sennacherib silver and gold. But Sennacherib sent a great army against King Hezekiah at Jerusalem (II Kg. 18:13-17). King Hezekiah cried to the LORD God for help and God spared the city of Jerusalem from the king of Assyria (II Kg. 19:32-37).

During the reign of King Jehoiachin (598 B. C.), King Nebuchadnezzar (605-562 B. C.) of Babylon Empire besieged Jerusalem. He carried off the treasure of the temple and of the palace. The king of Judah and his officials surrendered to the Babylonians. They were carried as prisoners to Babylon in ca. 598 B. C. They were about ten thousands (II Kg. 24:10-14). King Jehoiachin was replaced by Zedekiah (598-587 B. C.) as a king of Judah. When Zedekiah rebelled against King Nebuchadnezzar, Nebuchadnezzar besieged Jerusalem about a year in ca. 588 B. C. Zedekiah and his army tried to escape from the city. King Zedekiah was captured; his eyes were put out; and he was taken as a prisoner to Babylon. Again King Nebuchadnezzar entered Jerusalem; and burned down the temple and the city in 587 B. C.; and took people of Judah as captive to Babylon (II Kg. 25:8-21) in ca. 583 B. C. Thus, God used a foreign ruler to punish His people. The people of Israel remained in the captivity about seventy years, until the rise of the Persian Empire (II Chr. 36:20-21).

The main reason of the destruction of the kingdom of Judah was that the people sinned against the command of the LORD God. This was the cause of the destruction of the kingdom of Israel.

Ezra and Nehemiah were among the captives of Nebuchadnezzar. They were permitted to return to Jerusalem and rebuild the temple and the walls of Jerusalem by the Persian Emperors (II Chr. 36:23). God used King Cyrus (539-530 B. C.), a foreign ruler, to accomplish His purpose.

Conclusion

Ezra reviewed the spiritual history of the Jews from the call of Abraham to the return of the exiles in order to remind them of how his people acted stubbornly; and how God dealt with them graciously through those periods. Those periods had the features, which are mentioned in the analysis of the text, which need to be referred again in the conclusion.

(A) The people of Israel disobeyed the LORD God by worshipping other gods. Therefore, the wrath of God was kindled against them.

God abandoned His people for some time. He punished them through foreign rulers, who put the people of Israel under bondage or subjection.

(B) Then the people of Israel cried to the LORD God for their deliverance from the afflictions, inflicted by the foreign rulers. They repented of their sins and they asked God to forgive them. God heard their cry and raised leaders to save them from the afflictions.

(C) The people had rest from the afflictions for some time. They forgot what God had done for their deliverance from the foreign powers. They sinned against the LORD God by repeating their sins and made Him angry again.

(D) The people of Israel cried again to the LORD God for their deliverance from the foreign powers; and God delivered them many times according to His mercy and lovingkindness.

Ezra pointed out two spiritual things in his address: stubbornness of man or nation and lovingkindness of the LORD God. God kept His promise of saving His people despite His people rebelled against Him many times. He did not completely abandon His people. This is how God treats all nations, which would repent of their sins and turn to Him for salvation. We as a nation should repent of our collective sins; and ask God for forgiveness and salvation.

Recommended Hymns from the Methodist Hymnal

56 'Sweet is the memory of Thy grace,'

351 'I hear Thy welcome voice'

353 'Just as I am, without one plea'

498 'Rock of Ages, cleft for me,'

Recommended Responsive Reading from the Methodist Hymnal
35 (p. 398) or

69 (p.414),

Recommended Responsive Reading from *A Worship Manual for Scriptural or Methodist Order of Service*
28 (pp. 115-116) or

68 (pp. 174-175).

Endnotes

[1] *The New American Encyclopedia,* (Philadelphia / Munich: The Publishers Agency, Inc., 1974) Vol.12, pp. 4487-4488.

[2] Rev. Edward Jackman, *A Solar Seasonal Christian Calender,* (Toronto: Celtic Arts of Canada, 1990), p. 53.

[3] *The Interpreter's Bible,* (New York, Nashville: Abingdon-Cokesbury Press, 1952), Vol. I, p. 144.

Chapter 2

'Qualifications to Ascend the LORD's Hill,' 'Spiritual Requirement to be in the Presence of God,' 'Purity of Life as a Requirement.'

Scripture

Psalms 24:1-6

Exodus 3:4-6, 12; 19:4-6, 10-25; 33:17-23

Leviticus 11:44-45; 16:4, 6; 19:2; 20:26

Deuteronomy 12:5-6

II Samuel 6:12-19

I Chronicles 15:13

II Chronicles 7:15-16

Psalms 15:1-5

Matthew 5:8; 14:3

II Corinthians 6:16-7:1

Ephesians 4:17-24

I Peter 1:4, 13-16

II Peter 3:11-13

Text: Psalms 24:3-4

A Few Versions of the Text, Psalms 24:3-4

Who may ascend into the hill of the LORD? Or who may stand in His holy place? He who has clean hands and a pure heart, Who has not lifted up his soul to an idol, Not sworn deceitfully. *New King James Version*

Who may ascend into the hill of Jehovah? And who shall stand in his holy place? He that hath clean hands and a pure heart; who hath not lifted up his soul unto falsehood, And hath not sworn deceitfully. *The Wesleyan Bible Commentary*

Who shall ascend the hill of the LORD? And who shall stand in his holy place? He who has clean hands and a pure heart, who does not lift up his soul to what is false; and does not swear deceitfully. *Revised Standard Version*

Who may ascend into the hill of the LORD? Who may stand in his holy place? He who has clean hands and a pure heart, who has not lifted up his soul to an idol or swear by what is false. *New International Version*

Who may go up the mountain of the LORD? And who may stand in His holy place? He who has clean hands and a pure heart, who has not set his mind on falsehood, and has not committed perjury. *The New English Bible*

Who may climb the mountain of the Lord and enter where he lives? Who may stand before the Lord? Only those with pure hands and hearts, who do not practice dishonesty and lying. *The Living Bible Illustrated*

Who may go up the LORD's mountain? Who may stand in his holy place? The one who has clean hands and a pure heart and does not long for what is false or lie when he is under oath. *God's Word*

Introduction

The highest mountain in the world is Mount Everest. It was named after Sir George Everest (A. D.1790-1866), who was Surveyor General of India in 1830-1843 and completed a survey of Himalayan Mountains in 1841. Its height was computed to be 29,002 feets in 1860 by the Survey Department of India. The Chinese Department announced its height to be 29,032 feet in 1973.

Like Mount Everest, there are seventeen highest mountain peaks in the world. Fifteen of these mountain peaks were conquered between 1950 and 1960. Trisul is 23,364 feet high; it was conquered in 1907. Jongsong is 24, 344 feet high; it was conquered in 1930. Kamset is 25, 447 feet high; it was conquered in 1931.

People attempted to conquer Mount Everest. By World War II, three expeditions had reached 28,000 feet on the Mount Everest. Eleven persons from various preceding expeditions since 1921 died, who attempted to go on the top of Mount Everest. Edmund Hillary, a New Zealander, and his Sherpa guide, Tenzing Norkay, conquered the Mount Everest by climbing 29,028 feet on May 29, 1953.[1]

Mountain climbing is a very hard work. People, who attempt to go on the peaks of the mountains, have to be physically strong and mentally determined. The task of mountain climbing should be undertaken by those who are strong and tough; this work is not for the week and feeble.

Introduction of the Text

As mountain climbing is a hard task, it requires sound health, strong determination, and constant watchfulness. It needs help from others, who are in the team. In a similar way, a task of aspiring to be religious or spiritual demands exceptional determination; and it seeks help from God. This is a common experience of many devout believers. King David (1002-962 B. C.) echoed this common spiritual experience when he wrote the following verses:

Who shall ascend the hill of the LORD? And who shall stand in his holy place? He who has clean hands and a pure heart, who does not lift up his soul to what is false; and does not swear deceitfully. (Psalms 24: 3-4)

This is the text of our meditation now as we prepare ourselves for the Lenten Season.

The Context of the Text

Majority of the biblical scholars are of the opinion that King David wrote this Psalm 24 when he brought the ark of the covenant from the house of Obed-edom to the place which David had prepared for it in Jerusalem (II Sam. 6:12-19). King David had attempted to bring it to Zion before, carrying it upon a cart. Uzzah, a priest, tried to save the ark from falling to the ground. His unsancified action kindled the wrath of God, who killed Uzzah instantly. The expression of God's wrath against Uzzah made King David and his people particularly conscious of the holiness of God and of the ceremonial and moral cleanness necessary for those who would enter His presence. In his second attempt, King David carried the ark of God on the shoulders of the priests as God had ordained (I Chr. 15:13; Num. 7:9).[2]

The verses, Ps. 24:3-4, refer to the priests, who served in the tabernacle. The tabernacle was a tent where the ark of God was kept. The tabernacle was divided into sanctuary and the Holy of Holy place. The ark was kept in the Holy of Holy place. The priests were allowed to enter the sanctuary to discharge their priestly duties. Before they enter the sanctuary, they had to be ceremonially clean. Aaron, the high priest, was asked to bathe before he put the sacred garments- tunic, sash, and turban (Lev. 16:4). Then he had to offer two male goats for a sin offering, atonement offering for himself and for his household (Lev. 16:6). The sin offering was for a moral cleansing. Without the ceremonial and moral cleansing, the high priest and other priests were not allowed to be in the presence of God.

God is holy, therefore, He commanded His priests and the people to be holy, when He said to them: "For I am the LORD your God; consecrate yourselves therefore, and be holy, for I am holy." (Lev. 11:44,

45; 19:2; 20:26) It is the law of the holy God that no one should go into His presence without being holy or pure. This divinely prescribed code and practice was expressed when King David wrote these verses:

> Who shall ascend the hill of the LORD? And who shall stand in his holy place? He who has clean hands and a pure heart, who does not lift up his soul to what is false; and does not swear deceitfully. (Psalms 24:3-4)

This is the text, within its historical setting.

An Analysis of the Text

The verses of the text have three ideas.

(A) The first part of the third verse is a question, "Who shall ascend the hill of the LORD?"

(B) The second part of the same verse is a similar question, "And who shall stand in his holy place?"

(C) The fourth verse provides answers to those questions, stating: "He who has clean hands and a pure heart, who does not lift up his soul to what is false; and does not swear deceitfully."

An Exposition of the Ideas

(A) The first idea of the text is the question, "Who shall ascend the hill of the LORD?" The question implies that the LORD God resides on the hill, which is a sacred place. The presence or appearance of the LORD God on the hill or mountain makes the place holy. The God of the Bible is the God of mountain. Let us recall a few events to confirm the idea.

(1) Moses was keeping the flock on the Mount Horeb. He led the flock to west side of the wilderness of the Mount Horeb, which was the mountain of God. He saw a flame of fire out of the midst of a bush; but the bush was not being consumed by the fire. It was an unusual or strange site for him; therefore, he became curious to know about this extraordinary fact. When Moses approached the bush, God said to Moses:

> Moses, Moses, Do not come near, put off your shoes from your feet, for the place on which you are standing is holy ground. I am the God

of your father, the God of Abraham, the God of Isaac, and the God
of Jacob. (Ex. 3:4-6)

Moses heard the command of God; and in obedience he removed his
shoes from his feet. Then he hid his face, because he was afraid to look at
the face of God. Then God told Moses his mission to liberate His people
from the Egyptian bondage and affliction. The task of liberation was
very hard for Moses. Therefore, God gave Moses His assurance, saying:

> But I will be with you; and this shall be the sign for you, that I have sent
> you. When you have brought forth the people out of Egypt, you shall
> serve God upon this mountain. (Ex. 3:12)

(2) By God's help, Moses liberated the people of Israel from the Egyptian
bondage and led them to the wilderness of the Mount Sinai. God asked
Moses to come up or ascend the Mount Sinai. Then God told Moses to
deliver His message to the people, as follows:

> You have seen what I did to the Egyptians, and how I bore you on eagles'
> wings and brought you to myself. Now, therefore, if you will obey my
> voice and keep my covenant, you shall be my own possession among all
> peoples; for all the earth is mine, and you shall be to me a kingdom of
> priests and a holy notion. (Ex. 19:4-6)

Moses told God's message to the people; and they agreed to obey God.
Then God told Moses that on the third day, God would come down on
Mount Sinai in the sight of the people. God asked Moses to set bounds
for the people; and to tell them that they should wash their garments
and be clean; and they should not go up into the mountain or touch the
boarder of it or else they would be killed. Moses prepared the people
for the third day. On the third day, when God came on the mountain,
there were thunders and lightnings, a thick cloud; the whole mountain
was smoky.

The people were trembled to see the terrible scene. (Ex. 19:16-25)
This event teaches us that God's holiness is unique, unapproachable,
incomprehensible, and unattainable. Israel was not allowed to touch the
Mount Sinai. Israel trembled at His power; and it could not imagine
God's holiness.[3]

God's holiness is absolute; man can never attain it; man can never be holy as God is holy. God's holiness is absolute in the sense that He does not have to conform to the standard of holiness, because He Himself is the standard of holiness. He wants His people to conform to His standard. He said to His people, Israel:

> For I am the LORD who brought you up out of the land of Egypt, to be your God; you shall therefore be holy, for I am holy. (Lev. 11:45)

This commandment is repeated in Lev. 19:2. This commandment is enforced upon the Church, the new Israel. We shall deal with the point later on.

(3) Jesus Christ went up on a mountain; and gave a sermon or the new law of God to the people. (Mt. 5:1) He often went up to a mountain to be with God and to prayer. (Mt. 14:32)

From these evidences we can conclude that the God of the Bible is the God of mountain. Mountain is an abode of God. The people who want to be in the presence of God would have to climb the mountain.

(B) The second part of the same verse is a similar question, "And who shall stand in his holy place?" This question implies that the people would have to stand in the presence of holy God in order to worship Him and to offer sacrifices to Him. While the people of Israel were wandering in the wilderness, God said to them through Moses:

> But you shall seek the place which the LORD your God will choose out of all your tribes to put his name and make his habitation there; thither you shall go, and thither you shall bring your burnt offerings, and your sacrifices, your tithes and the offering that you present, your votive offerings, your freewill offerings, and the firstlings of your herd and of your flock. (Deut. 12:5-6; cf. Deut. 12:11-14; 14:23; 15:20; 16:2; 17:8)

That place of worship and sacrifices was the first temple, built by King Solomon (962-922 B. C.) (II Chr. 7: 15-16). The temple was patterned in accordance with the tabernacle. The temple had the inner sanctuary or the Holy of Holies. God consecrated the temple as His place of abode.

Only the high priest was allowed to enter inner sanctuary once a year, on the day of atonement, after he had cleansed himself ceremonially and morally. Other priests were allowed to function in the sanctuary, when they purified themselves ceremonially and morally. Other people were not allowed to enter the sanctuary, because they were not considered to be as holy as the priests. The priests were permitted to offer sacrifices on behalf of the people. They were allowed to stand in the sanctuary to offer sacrifices to God.

(**C**) The fourth verse provides answers to those questions, stating: "He who has clean hands and a pure heart, who does not lift up his soul to what is false; and does not swear deceitfully." In other words, a person, who has clean hands or who does not do evil things, or whose deeds are righteous, who is truthful, shall be allowed to climb the holy mountain of God and to stand in the presence of holy God. The evil and deceitful people were not worthy to be in the presence of God; only the righteous people were worthy to enter in the presence of God. The practice of godly righteousness is a requirement to be in presence of God. This idea was very important; therefore, King David reiterated the idea in another psalm, as follows:

> O LORD, who shall sojourn in thy tent? Who shall dwell on thy holy hill? He who walks blamelessly, and does what is right, and speaks truth from his heart; who does not slander with his tongue, and does no evil to his friend, nor takes up a reproach against his neighbour; in whose eyes a reprobate is despised, but who honours those who fear the LORD; who swears to his own hurt and does not change; who does not put his money at interest, and does not take a bribe against the innocent. He who does these things shall never be removed. (Ps. 15:1-5)

The people, who practice righteousness, honesty, and integrity, would be allowed to stand in the presence of God and God would establish them as His people.

Christians are the new Israel, the chosen people of God. They are addressed as saints, the holy ones, in the New Testament. The believers of the early Church were not very righteous persons nor they had extraordinary piety. They were ordinary people, who were set apart and called for purity. Latin phrase for saints is *simul justus et peccator*; this phrase means 'at the same time just and sinner.'[4] It means a Christian is just and sinner at the same time. How can we understand this apparent contradiction? When a sinner believes in the atoning blood of Jesus Christ, the sinner is saved by His faith in the grace of Jesus Christ. This is called justification by faith. When a person is justified, God transfers righteousness of Jesus Christ to the account of the saved person. Justness of Jesus Christ becomes the property of the saved person. This transaction is real for believers. When the believers are covered and clothed by the righteousness of Jesus Christ, God treats them as just or righteous people.

God has given the believers many instructions through His Word as to how they can lead a moral and spiritually pure life. They are expected to lead their life according to those instructions. Leading a moral and spiritually pure life on this earth entitles the believers to see the holy God in their heavenly life. The believers have to prepare for the heavenly fitness here and now. St. Peter mentioned the divine inheritance of Christians, describing it as 'imperishable, undefiled, unfading, kept in heaven.' (I Pet. 1:4) He exhorted Christians to aspire for it, saying:

> Therefore gird up your minds, be sober, set your hope fully upon the grace that is coming to you at the revelation of Jesus Christ. As obedient children, do not be conformed to the passions of your former ignorance, but as he who called you is holy, be holy yourselves in all your conduct; since it is written, 'You shall be holy, for I am holy.' (I Pet. 1:13-16)

St. Peter repeated this exhortation in his second letter, as follows:

> Since all these things are thus to be dissolved, what sort of persons ought you to be in lives of holiness and godliness, waiting for and hastening the coming of the day of God, because of which the heavens will be kindled and dissolved, and the elements will melt with fire! But according to his promise we wait for new heavens and a new earth in which righteousness dwells. (II Pet. 3:11-13)

In these words, St. Peter asked the believers to lead holy life in order to be in the new heavens and the new earth.

Without referring to this eschatological hope, St. Paul exhorted Christians at Corinth to lead a holy life, in these words:

> For we are the temple of the living God; as God said, 'I will live in them and move among them, and I will be their God, and they shall be my people. Therefore come out from them, and be separate from them, says the Lord, and touch nothing unclean; then I will welcome you and I will be a father to you, and you shall be my sons and daughters, says the Lord Almighty.' Since we have these promises, beloved, let us cleanse ourselves from every defilement of body and spirit, and make holiness perfect in the fear of God. (II Cor. 6:16-7:1)

In a similar way, St. Paul wrote to the Christians at Ephesus, as follows:

> Now this I affirm and testify in the Lord, that you must no longer live as the Gentiles do, in the futility of their minds; they are darkened in their understanding, alienated from the life of God because of their ignorance that is in them, due to their hardness of heart; they have become callous and have given themselves up to licentiousness, greedy to practise every kind of uncleanness. You did not so learn Christ! - assuming that you have heard about him and were taught in him, as the truth is in Jesus. Put off your old nature which belongs to your former manner of life and is corrupt through deceitful lusts, and be renewed in the spirit of your minds, and put on the new nature, created after the likeness of God in the righteousness and holiness. (Eph. 4:17-24)

Conclusion

Believers in Jesus Christ should aspire to be holy and righteous people because their God is holy and righteous. Let their hearts be pure. Without the purity of heart, they will not be able to see God, as Jesus said, "Blessed are the pure in heart, for they shall see God." (Mt. 5:8) Without holiness, believers will not be allowed to stand in the presence of the Lord God.

Walking in holiness is a hard task, like climbing a peak of a mountain. Therefore King David wrote the words of the text, which we have been meditating:

> Who shall ascend the hill of the LORD? And who shall stand in his holy place? He who has clean hands and a pure heart, who does not lift up his soul to what is false; and does not swear deceitfully. (Psalms 24:3-4)

These words do not only apply to the priests, who were serving God in holiness, but they also apply to all believers who aspire to be in the presence of the holy God for ever.

Recommended Hymns from the Methodist Hymnal

87 'Jesus comes with all His grace,'

498 'Rock of Ages, cleft for me,'

547 'The thing my God doth hate'

557 'What is our calling's glorious hope'

565 'I know that my Redeemer lives,

697 'Blest are the humble souls that see'

Recommended Responsive Reading from the Methodist Hymnal
26 (p. 393),

Recommended Responsive Reading from *A Worship Manual for Scriptural or Methodist Order of Service*:
19 (p.102).

Hymn # 544 form the Methodist Hymnal to be used as invocation.

Endnotes
[1] Paul Lee Tan, *Encyclopedia of 7700 Illustrations: Signs of the Times*, # 3718, 3723.

[2] *The Wesleyan Bible Commentary*, Vol. Two, p. 230.

[3] A. W. Tozer, *The Knowledge of the Holy*, (India: Alliance Publications, 1961), p. 128.

[4] R. C. Sproul, *The Holiness of God*, (Illinois: Tyndale Publisher, 1985), p. 212.

Chapter 3

'A Necessity of a Right Spirit,' 'A Necessity of a Clean Heart,' 'God Creates a New and Right Spirit within Man,' 'Religion of a Clean Heart.'

Scripture

Psalms 51:1-17

Genesis 1:3-25

Exodus 20:14, 17

II Samuel 11:10-11; 12:5-6, 7-12, 13-14

Psalms 61:6

Ezekiel 36:26-27

II Corinthians 7:1

II Timothy 2:21-22

James 4:8

I John 1:9

Text: Psalms 51:10

A Few Versions of the Text, Psalms 51:10

Create in me a clean heart, O God, And renew a steadfast spirit within me. *The New King James Version*

Create in me a clean heart, O God; And renew a right spirit within me. *Wesleyan Bible Commentary*

Create in me a clean heart, O God, and put a new and right spirit within me. *Revised Standard Version*

Create in me a pure heart, O God, and renew a steadfast spirit within me. *New International Version*

Create a pure heart in me, O God, and give me a new and steadfast spirit; *The New English Bible*

Create in me a new, clean heart, O God, filled with clean thoughts and right desires. *The Living Bible Illustrated*

Create a clean heart in me, O God, and renew a faithful spirit within me. *God's word*

Introduction

Biblical religion is different from other world religions. Some religions, like Islam, Hinduism, lay emphasis on ritualism and sacrifices as means of salvation. For example, one of the pillars of Islam is to do *hajj* or to go on pilgrimage to Mecca and Medina, the holy cities in Saudi Arabia. If a Muslim goes for a pilgrimage, Allah, the god of Islam, forgives all kinds of sins, such as adultery, murder, cheating, and lying, even if the pilgrim does not repent of his sins. Similarly, Hindus believe that they should bathe in the river Ganges on an auspicious day (viz. *Kumbhamela)* in order to get forgiveness of all kinds of sins, even without true repentance. This belief of Muslims and Hindus ignore purity of heart or being born again spiritually. But the biblical religions such as,

Judaism and Christianity, do not consider rituals as means of salvation. King David, in a psalm, wrote:

> For thou [the LORD God] hast no delight in sacrifice; were I to give a burnt offering, thou wouldst not be pleased. The sacrifice acceptable to God is a broken spirit; a broken and contrite heart, O God, thou wilt not despise. (Ps. 51:16-17)

Christianity believes the doctrine that salvation is by grace of God; and man must repent of his sins and keep his heart pure, after being saved by God's grace in Jesus Christ. Christianity and Judaism are the religions of heart. And every believer is expected to have a clean heart or to walk in holiness. If the hearts are filled with filthiness or wickedness, action will be wicked and sinful. But if, on the other hand, hearts are pure or clean, actions will be really righteous. Our spiritual well-being depends on good actions and good intentions.

The writer of the Book of Proverbs realized a necessity of clean heart; therefore, he wrote:

> Keep your heart with all vigilance; for from it flow the springs of life. (Pr. 4:23)

In other words, we have to protect our hearts from evil influence with all alertness, because our hearts are the springs of life. We aspire to have the eternal life by the grace of God. If our hearts are not filled with purity and morality, we are doomed for eternal divine punishment or for death and destruction.

Introduction of the Text

King David (1002-962 B. C.) committed some sins, because his heart was filled with lust and worldly pleasures. God told him through prophet Nathan God's punishment for his sins. He realized the gravity of his sins; therefore, he repented of his sins. He prayed to the LORD God:

> **Create in me a clean heart, O God, and put a new and right spirit within me. (Psalms 51:10)**

This is the text of our meditation now.

The Context of the Text

The words of the text are taken from the Psalm 51. The historical background of this psalm is given in II Samuel 11. According to this chapter, David was a king of Israel. He was a powerful king. In the ancient world, all kings had absolute power and authority. All people were subjected to kings. People had to satisfy all wishes and whims of their kings. King David had such an absolute power and authority over the people of Israel.

King David was a great warrior; he had fought many fights with the Philistines and the Ammorites. It was an established practice in the ancient world that kings had to lead battles. In the spring of a year, King David did not go with his army on the battlefield. He remained at his palace in Jerusalem. He sent Joab, the commander of his army, and other soldiers to fight against the Ammorites. While other soldiers were engaged in the battle with the Ammorites, King David was relaxing and enjoying life. He arose from his couch; and was walking on the terrace of his palace, late one afternoon. He saw from the terrace a very beautiful woman, bathing herself. It was a fascinating scene for King David. That fascination led him to temptation. King David wanted that beautiful woman for his pleasure. He inquired about the woman, called Bathsheba. He was told that she was the wife of Uriah the Hittite. He was also told that Uriah the Hittite was a loyal soldier, who was on the battlefield. King David's heart was so much filled with lust and passion that he lost the sight of moral values and the fear of God. He wanted Bathsheba at any cost. He must have ignored God's two commandments, namely, 'You shall not commit adultery' (Ex. 20:14) and 'you shall not covet your neighbour's wife, or his manservant, or his maid servant, or his ox, or his ass, or anything that is your neighbours.' (Ex. 20:17)

As King David had ignored God's commandments, he sent messengers to Bathsheba and brought her in his palace. He slept with her; he defiled the wife of his royal solider and neighbour. King David exercised his absolute royal power and authority for a wrong purpose, that is, to commit an adultery with someone's wife.

David slept with Bathsheba, after she purified herself from her uncleanness, due to her monthly course. Having satisfied his lust, King David sent her to her house. After a few months, Bathsheba sent a message to King David that she was pregnant.

King David was facing a problem as to how to avoid consequences. He wanted to cover his wrong doing, his sin. He thought that if Bathsebha's husband would sleep with her, her pregnancy could be ascribed to their union; and then he (King David) could be free from his sin. He sent a word to Joab to send Uriah the Hittite to his home in Jerusalem. Then King David asked Uriah to see his wife. But Uriah did not go home; he slept in the palace. When King David came to know that Uriah did not go home to see his wife, King David asked him, "Have you not come from a journey? Why did you not go down to your house?" (II Sam. 11:10) Uriah, who was very loyal to the code of ethics, said to King David:

> The ark and Israel and Judah swell in boots; and my lord Joab and the servants of my lord are camping in the open field; shall I then go to my house, to eat and drink, and lie with my wife? As you live, and as your soul lives, I will not do this thing. (II Sam. 11:11)

In these words, Uriah expressed his moral position that he should not enjoy life, but suffer with other fellow soldiers. King David did not like his answer, because it was a right judgment on King David, who was enjoying life while others were risking their life on the battlefield.

King David's words did not convince Uriah to go home and see his wife. Then King David asked Uriah to eat and drink with him next day. King David made Uriah drunk, hoping that Uriah would go to see his wife, because he was under an influence of alcohol. Uriah became drunk; but he did not lose the sense of right and wrong. His sense of loyalty and integrity kept him away from enjoying his wife. He slept at the palace. Thus, King David's trick failed.

In order to save himself from embarrassment and disgrace, King David made a plot to get rid of Uriah so that he could have his wife Bathsebha. He wrote a note to Joab, the commander, as to how he should get Uriah killed. Joab obeyed King David's order. Uriah was killed in a fierce battle. Uriah did not die alone; but other soldiers were also killed in the battle.

When Bathsebha heard that her husband was killed in the battle, she lamented for him, because she was loving him sincerely. After the days of mourning, King David brought Bathshebha in his palace; and she gave birth to a son.

King David was very happy, because he had another son; and also he was successful to have a very beautiful wife. While King David was enjoying his family life, the LORD God was displeased with King David because of his sins: committing adultery, coveting his neighbour's wife, plotting to kill Uriah, and letting other soldiers to be killed with Uriah. He was blood guilty and an adulterer in the sight of the LORD God. The LORD God sent prophet Nathan to King David with a message and judgment. Nathan told the parable of a rich man, who had many flocks and herds, and a poor man, who had one little lamb. The poor man was loving the lamb very much. When the rich man had to give a feast to his friends, the rich man took away the poor man's lamb and made a feast. When King David heard the story, he became very angry against the rich man. King David said to prophet Nathan in his judgement on the event, as follows:

> As the LORD lives, the man who has done this deserves to die; and he shall restore the lamb fourfold, because he did this thing, and because he had no pity. (II Sam. 12:5-6)

King David was very quick to condemn the sinful man; but in his own judgment he was judged. When prophet Nathan heard the judgment from the lips of King David, he said to King David:

> You are the man. Thus says the LORD, the God of Israel, 'I anointed you king over Israel, and delivered you out of the hand of Saul; and I gave you your master's house, and your master's wives into your bosom,

and gave you the house of Israel and of Judah; and if this were too little, I would add to you as much more. Why have you despised the word of the LORD, to do what is evil in his sight? You have smitten Uriah the Hittite with the sword, and have taken his wife to be your wife, and have slain him with the sword of the Ammonites. Now therefore the sword shall never depart from your house, because you have despised me, and have taken the wife of Uriah the Hittite to be your wife.' Thus says the LORD, 'Behold, I will raise up evil against you out of your own house; and I will take your wives before your eyes, and give them to your neighbour, and he shall lie with your wives in the sight of this sun. For you did it secretly but I will do this thing before all Israel, and before the sun. (II Sam 12:7-12)

Then King David said to prophet Nathan 'I have sinned against the LORD.' (II Sam. 12:13) He said it with a repentant heart. Then prophet Nathan told King David that God had forgiven his sins; but his child, born out of sin, would die. (II Sam.12:13-14)

King David's conversation with prophet Nathan reflected his repentance. The spirit of King David's repentance is expressed in his psalm, as follows:

For I know my transgressions, and my sin is ever before me. Against thee, thee only, have I sinned, and done that which is evil in thy sight, so that thou are justified in the sentence and blameless in thy judgment. Behold, I was brought forth in iniquity, and in sin did my mother conceive me. (Ps. 51:3-5)

Then King David sincerely and contritely asked the LORD God to purge him and to purify him, saying:

Purge me with hyssop, and I shall be clean; wash me, and I shall be whiter than snow... Create in me a clean heart, O God, and put a new and right spirit within. Deliver me from bloodguiltiness, O God. (Ps. 53:7, 10, 14)

The text of our meditation, "Create in me a clean heart, O God, and put a new and right spirit within." appears in this historical background.

An Analysis of the Text

This text has only one idea. King David prayed to the LORD God to create in him a clean heart or to put a new and right spirit within him.

A clean heart is similar to a new and right spirit. These two expressions are synonymous.

An Exposition of the Ideas of the Text

King David asked the LORD God to create in him a clean or pure heart. Man can repair, redesign, and renovate things; but he has no ability to create a new thing. The power of creation belongs to God only. God creates something out of nothing. God's act of creation does not depend on any thing. He speaks and at His word the things are created. (Gen. 1:3-25) King David knew God's power of creation.

King David asked God to create in him a clean or pure heart, because his heart, the inward being of man (Ps. 61:6) was defiled by a chain of evil deeds he committed in order to have Bathsheba his wife. He committed adultery with Bathsebha; he used devious means to cover his act of adultery; he caused Uriah the Hittite and other soldiers to be killed in the battlefield. He ignored God's commandments in order to satisfy an urge of his lust and passion. His heart was gradually becoming defiled. He became insensitive to sins or his heart became the heart of stone. He forgot God and His commandments. King David asked God to put a new and right spirit within him, because his old spirit became wrong or failing spirit. He asked God to give him right or steadfast or unfailing heart.

If a man or a woman asks of God to give him or her a new heart, as King David asked, God would promise him or her, as He did before, in these words:

> A new heart I will give you, a new spirit I will put within you; and I will take out of your flesh the heart of stone and give you a heart of flesh. And I will put my spirit within you, and cause you to walk in my statutes and be careful to observe my ordinances. (Ezek. 36:26-27)

God wants people to have a new heart so that they would be right within and right without. He wants to give them a new spirit so that they would be right with Him and right with others. God wants the people to walk in His way. He wants to remove man's stone heart, the heart which has become insensitive to sins and guilt, and to give the heart of flesh to be concerned with the legitimate rights of others.

Similar teaching is found in the New Testament. St. James wrote:

Draw near to God and he will draw near to you. Cleanse your hands, you sinners, and purify your hearts, you men of double mind. (Jas. 4:8)

Double mindedness creates confusion, hypocrisy, and ill feelings. Therefore such a mind should be removed and replaced by a pure or sincere heart.

Like St. James, St. Paul wrote:

If any one purifies himself from what is ignoble, then he will be a vessel for noble use, consecrated and useful to the master of the house, ready for any good work. So shun youthful passions and aim at righteousness, faith, love, and peace, along with those who call upon the Lord from a pure heart. (II Tim 2:21-22)

The LORD God wants the believers to be His people and to be their God. God has made a new covenant with Christians. In this context, St. Paul wrote to the church at Corinth:

Since we have these promises, behold, let us cleanse ourselves from every defilement of body and spirit, and make holiness perfect in the fear of God. (II Cor. 7:1)

Conclusion

God is able to cleanse the believers and others from all unrighteousness (I Jn 1:9), from all sins, and from all spiritual defilements; but He wants us to say to Him as sincerely as King David said:

Create in me a clean (or pure) heart, O God, and put a new and right (or steadfast) spirit within me. (Ps. 51:10)

Is everyone prepared to say these words to God now; and to walk in His holy and perfect path? Remember the basic teaching of the Bible that there is no forgiveness of sins without a repentant or contrite heart, because a repentant heart guarantees a sure walk with God, a walk of rightness and moral purity, after repentance. God cannot be deceived or mocked by any person.

May this Lenten season be a season of holiness and righteousness for us and for all believers. Amen!

Recommended Hymns from the Methodist Hymnal:
36 'Holy, holy, holy, Lord God Almighty!'

241 'O Son of Man, our hero strong and tender,'

351 'I hear Thy welcome voice'

492 'I the good fight have fought,'

498 'Rock of Ages, cleft for me'

744 'I am Thine, O Lord, I have heard'

Recommended Responsive Reading from the Methodist Hymnal:
35 (p. 398)

Recommended Responsive Reading from *A Worship Manual for Scriptural or Methodist Order of Service:*
28 (pp.115-116).

Chapter 4

'The Source of Help'
'The Creator, the Source of Help.'
'Looking Upward to the Hill of the LORD'

Scripture

Psalms 121:1-8

Exodus 3:7-10, 12; 19:1-2; 20: 4-6; 23: 14-17; 34:22-23

Leviticus 23:1-44

Deuteronomy 4: 15-19; 16:1-7

I Kings 18: 21, 36-37, 40

Psalms 28:6-8; 53:1-3; 118:8-9

Proverbs 20:9

Isaiah 24:23; 31:1; 36:4-6; 41:8-10; 53:6; 64:6

Jeremiah 3:23; 17:5-8

Romans 3:23

Hebrews 12:18-24; 13:6

I John 1:8

Text: Psalms 121:1-2

A Few Versions of the Text, Psalms 121:1-2

I will lift up my eyes to the hill- From whence comes my help? My help comes from the LORD, Who made heaven and earth. *New King James Version*

I will lift up mine eyes unto the mountain: From whence shall my help come? My help cometh from Jehovah, who made heaven and earth. *The Wesleyan Bible Commentary*

I lift up my eyes to the hills. From whence does my help come? My help comes from the LORD, who made heaven and earth. *Revised Standard Version*

I lift up my eyes to the hills- where does my help come from? My help comes from the LORD, the maker of heaven and earth. *New International Version*

If I lift up my eyes to the hills, where shall I find help? Help comes only from the LORD, maker of heaven and earth. *The New English Bible*

Shall I look to the mountain gods for help? No! My help is from Jehovah who made the mountains! And the heavens too! *The Living Bible Illustrated*

I look up towards the mountains. Where can I find help? My help comes from the LORD, the maker of heaven and earth. *God's Word*

Introduction

Mountains attract attention of human beings because of their sizes and heights. In the ancient world, forts were built on the mountains to protect the villages from the attacks of enemies. Mountains provided protection to the people. Whenever there were floods on the plain lands, people flew to the mountains to take shelters from floods. For these reasons, mountains had obtained their useful significance.

Introduction of the Text

Mountains have obtained significance not only from physical perspective but they have obtained an additional significance from a spiritual perspective. A psalm writer states this perspective in the following words:

I lift up my eyes to the hills. From whence does my help come? My help comes from the LORD, who made heaven and earth. (Psalms 121:1-2)

This is the text of our meditation now.

The Context of the Text

The words of the text are taken form one of the psalms which are called 'songs of ascents.' These songs of ascents are put together in the section of Psalms from 120 to 134. These songs of the ascents talk about religious experience of the pilgrims, who were climbing the hills of Zion or Jerusalem.

The people of Israel were commanded by God to appear three times in a year before Him to observe feasts (Ex. 34:22-23; 23:14-17; Lev. 23:1-44; Deut. 16:1-7). These feasts are called 'pilgrim feasts.' The names of these pilgrim feasts are: (1) The feast of unleavened bread, (2) The feast of harvest, and (3) The feast of ingathering at the end of the year (Ex. 23:14-17). These feasts were observed at the central temple in Jerusalem.

The pilgrim, who wished to participate in the 'pilgrim feasts' had to climb the hill or mountains, surrounding Zion or Jerusalem. The pilgrim used to sing these songs of ascents, while they were climbing the mountains. Singing of those hymns refreshed their tired bodies and souls. A psalm writer, who was going to Jerusalem for these feasts, told his spiritual experience in these words:

I lift up my eyes to the hills. From whence does my help come? My help comes from the LORD, who made heaven and earth. (Ps. 121:1-2)

This is the text within its historical setting.

An Analysis of the Text

This text has two ideas. (A) The first idea is that the psalm writer talks about his spiritual habit of lifting his eyes to the hills, from which he receives his help.

(B) The second idea further clarifies who is the source of his help; the psalm writer states that he receives his help from the LORD, the maker of heaven and earth.

An Exposition of the Ideas of the Text

(A) The first idea is that the psalm writer talks about his spiritual habit of lifting his eyes to the hills, from which he receives his help. It means that whenever the psalmist had problems, difficulties, or crises in his life, he looked toward the hills of Zion or Jerusalem for help. He looked heavenward or above for the help. He did not look around, look down, and look within for help.

(1) First, the psalmist did not look around for the help. He did not go to his relatives, friends, counsellors, advisors, and psychiatrist for the help to solve his problems. The humans can be helpful to some extent; and they can provide a limited help. However, they cannot be helpful for all the problems and at all times. The word of God does not encourage anyone to trust in man, however that man may be mighty. A psalm writer says:

> It is better to take refuge in the LORD than to put confidence in man. It
> is better to take refuge in the LORD than to put confidence in princes.
> (Ps. 118: 8-9)

Prophet Isaiah advised the kings of Judah not to trust in other kings but to trust in the Lord, when he wrote:

> Woe to those who go down to Egypt for help and rely on horses, who
> trust in chariots because they are many and in horsemen because they
> are very strong, but do not look to the Holy One of Israel or consult the
> LORD. (Is. 31:1 cf. Is. 36:4-6)

Prophet Jeremiah gave the similar message in the name of God, when he said:

> Thus says the LORD: ' Cursed is the man who trusts in man and makes flesh his arm, whose heart turns away from the LORD. He is like a shrub in the desert, and shall not see any good come. He shall dwell in the parched places of the wilderness, in an uninhabited salt land. Blessed is the man who trusts in the LORD, whose trust is in the LORD. He is like a tree planted by water, that sends out its roots by the stream, and does not fear when heat comes, for its leaves remain green, and is not anxious in the year of drought for it does not cease to bear fruit.' (Jer. 17: 5-8)

(2) Secondly, the psalmist did not look down for the help; he did not look toward subhuman nature for help. He did not go to the trees and animals to ask for help. He did not ask the big trees, cows, snakes, dogs to help him. Some people in the world worship plants and animals, believing that the spirits of those animals and plants would help them. Further, some people worship stones and mountains, the inanimate things, because they believe that the spirits of gods abide in them. When man worship animate beings and inanimate things, which are subhuman, man degrades himself. Man is made in the image of God (Gen. 1:26-27) and he should maintain his spiritual dignity.

Worship of inanimate things and animate beings is against the worship of God, the creator of the heaven and the earth. He commanded the people of Israel to worship Him alone, saying:

> You shall not make for yourself a graven image, or any likeness of anything that is in heaven above, or that is in the earth beneath, or that is in the water under the earth; you shall not bow down to them or serve them; for I the LORD your God am a jealous God, visiting the iniquity of the fathers upon the children to the third and the fourth generation of those who hate me, but showing steadfast love to those who love me and keep my commandments. (Ex. 20:4-6)

This commandment is expanded in the Book of Deuteronomy, in the following words:

> Therefore take good heed to yourselves. Since you saw no form on the day that the LORD spoke to you at Horeb out of the midst of the fire, beware lest you act corruptly by making a graven image for yourselves, in

> the form of any figure, the likeness of any beast that is on the earth, the likeness of any winged bird that flies in the air, the likeness of anything that creeps on the ground, the likeness of any fish that is in water under the earth. And beware lest you lift up your eyes to heaven, and when you see the sun and the moon and the stars, all the hosts of heaven, you be drawn away and worship them and serve them, things which the LORD your God has allotted to all the people under the whole heaven. (Deut.4:15-19)

(3) Thirdly, the psalmist did not look within himself for help; he knew that he cannot help himself. He was fully aware of his sinful nature; he knew that all people are sinful and none of them is righteous before God. A psalm writer describes the sinful nature of all, in these words:

> They are corrupt, doing abominable iniquity; there is none that does good. God looks down from heaven upon the sons of men to see if there are any that are wise, that seek after God. They have fallen away; they are alike depraved; there is none that does good, no, not one. (Ps. 53:1-3)

Prophet Isaiah affirmed the universal sinful nature of all (Is. 53:6). All are affected by sin. He said:

> We have all become like one who is unclean, and all our righteous deeds are like a polluted garment. We all fade like a leaf, and our iniquities, like the wind, take us away. (Is. 64:6)

The writer of the book of Proverbs challenged anyone who would claim to be pure, when he wrote these words:

> Who can say, 'I have made my heart clean; I am pure from my sin?' (Pr. 20:9)

Having quoted the verses from the Old Testament (Rom. 3:10-18), St. Paul endorsed the idea of universality of sin, when he wrote: "Since all have sinned and fall short of the glory of God." (Rom. 3:23) Similarly apostle John reaffirmed this idea. (I Jn 1:8)

(B) The second idea further clarifies who is the source of his help; the psalm writer states that he receives his help from the LORD, the maker of heaven and earth. The psalm writer looks up toward the hills of Zion, from which he receives help. This thought might suggest that the psalm writer was a worshipper of the hills of Zion as the heathens.

Therefore, he immediately clarifies that he receives the help from the maker of heaven and earth.

The hills of Zion, where the temple of the LORD God was situated, were the holy hills for the psalm writer. Those holy hills represent other mountains, where the events of salvation or liberation took place, and where the glory and power of God were manifested. Let us remind ourselves of those events, and their association with the mountains.

(1) Moses became a great leader of Hebrews; he brought Hebrews out of the Egyptian slavery and gave them political, social, and religious freedom. He personally was not capable to do this tremendous task. It was God who was the author of the freedom of Hebrews.

Moses was brought up in the palace of the Pharaoh. He was born during the time when Hebrew male children were ordered to be killed by nurses. God spared the life of Moses. Moses, in his prime youth, realized that he was born of slave parents. He had been observing how Hebrew slaves were treated by the Egyptians. He wished to protect his kinsmen with his might. On one occasion, he killed an Egyptian who was fighting with a Hebrew. The news of this event spread among Hebrews and Egyptians. This made his staying in Egypt precarious. He became afraid of being tried by the Egyptian authority and be sentenced. He left Egypt and went to Midian to live in seclusion, where he was asked to look after the flock of his father-in-law. While he was feeding the flock on the mount Horeb, he saw a burning bush. He approached the burning bush; and God spoke to him through the bush. God assigned him the leadership of Hebrews, when He said:

> I have seen the affliction of my people who are in Egypt, and have heard their cry because of their taskmasters; I know their sufferings, and I have come down to deliver them out of the hand of the Egyptians... Come, I will send you to Pharaoh that you may bring forth my people, the sons of Israel, out of Egypt. (Ex. 3:7-10)

Moses was not happy and willing to accept the divine commission, because the task was herculean. God had to convince Moses to accept the task, assuring Moses that He would be with him in accomplishing the task. Moses returned to Egypt to tell Pharaoh and Hebrews that God had sent him to liberate Hebrews from the Egyptian bondage. Moses had to face trials and frustrations, but he did not give up the task. He depended on God's help in the times of crises and God helped him always. Moses did ten miracles with God's help and convinced the Egyptians and their Pharaoh, Ramses II (1301-1234 B. C.) that God was behind those plagues. Finally, Hebrews were allowed to leave Egypt, after 1300 B. C. Moses led Hebrews through the wilderness to the mountain, where God had previously appeared to him in the burning bush (Ex. 3:12; 19:1-2).

(2) Prophet Elijah was able to stop the widespread worship of the Baal and bring back the people of Israel to worship the LORD God. This was a difficult task. God was with Elijah to accomplish the task.

King Ahab (869-850 B. C.) and his wife Jezebel patronized the Baal worship, which was a fertility cult and a form of sympathetic magic. The Baal worship was becoming popular; and the people of Israel neglected to worship God Yahweh. Prophet Elijah became worried over popular worship of the Baal. His task was to bring back the people of Israel to worship the LORD God. His task was difficult because it would present a challenge to the king and the queen. But Elijah was determined to accomplish the task. He summoned all people of Israel, four hundred and fifty priests of Baal, and four hundred prophets of goddess Asherah, to be gathered on the mount Carmel. He challenged them, saying:

> How long will you go limping with two different opinions? If the LORD
> is God, follow him; but if Baal, then follow him. (I Kg. 18:21)

Prophet Elijah asked the people to make a choice definitely. He then asked the priests of the Baal to kill a bull and lay it up on wood without setting fire and invoke their gods to consume the sacrifice. The priests of the Baal went on crying till evening, but nothing happened. Then in the evening Elijah killed a bull and made an altar; he asked the people to pour water on the sacrifice. Then he invoked the LORD God, saying:

> O LORD, God of Abraham, Isaac, and Israel, let it be known this day
> that thou art God in Israel, and that I am thy servant, and that I have
> done all these things at thy word. Answer me, O LORD, answer me, that
> this people may know that thou, O LORD, art God, and that thou hast
> turned their hearts back. (I Kg. 18:36-37)

Then fire fell from heaven and consumed the sacrifice. God Yahweh proved Himself to be the true and powerful God on the mount Carmel. Being convinced of the power of God, at the command of prophet Elijah, people captured the priests of Baal and Asherah and killed them (I Kg. 18:40).

(3) Mount Sinai or Mount Horeb and Mount Carmel are thought to be holy mountains because the LORD God appeared on those mountains to manifest His power and to give deliverance to the people. Mount Zion is considered to be a holy mountain, because God's city, Zion or Jerusalem, is situated on it. Prophet Isaiah explained why Mount Zion is holy, in the following words:

> The LORD of hosts has become king on Mount Zion and in Jerusalem,
> and shows his glory before their elders. (Is. 24:23)

Mount Sinai, Mount Carmel, and Mount Zion are considered to be holy only because the LORD God manifested His power and glory on those mountains. Reverence to these mountains is due not because of their heights and sizes but because God appeared on these mountains. Prophet Jeremiah made this point clear to the people of Israel, when he said:

> There is no help in worship on the hill-tops, no help from clamour on the
> heights; truly in the LORD our God is Israel's only salvation. (Jer. 3:23)

The psalmist looked up the hills of Zion not because of their heights but because the LORD God appeared on them. The Lord God is the maker of heaven and earth; and He gives help to those who cry to Him.

The writers of the Bible bore witness that God helped them. King David wrote:

> Blessed be the LORD! For he has heard the voice of my supplications.
> The LORD is my strength and my shield; in him my heart trusts; so I
> am helped, and my heart exults, and with my song I give thanks to him.

> The LORD is the strength of his people, he is the saving refuge of his anointed. (Ps. 28:6-8 cf. Ps. 27:9; 40:17)

The LORD God assured His help to the exiled people of Israel through prophet Isaiah in the following words:

> But you, Israel, my servant, Jacob, whom I have chosen, the offspring of Abraham, my friend; you whom I took from the ends of the earth, and called you from its farthest corners, saying to you, 'You are my servant, I have chosen you and not cast you off;' fear not, for I am with you, be not dismayed, for I am your God; I will strengthen you, I will help you, I will uphold you with my victorious right hand. (Is. 41: 8-10)

The Lord God in Jesus Christ had been with His servants; He gave them courage to face persecutions and crises. The writer of the Letter to the Hebrews affirmed this confidence, saying:

> Hence we can confidently say, 'The Lord is my helper, I will not be afraid; what can man do to me?' (Heb. 13:6)

The Lord God always helped His servants, whenever they cried to Him for help; therefore, they developed a habit to look toward the LORD for help in the face of crises. Their habit to look up toward the LORD is the same as the habit of the psalm writer.

Conclusion

Mount Sinai, Mount Carmel, and Mount Zion are holy mountains, because the events of salvation took place on them. Jesus Christ manifested the work of redemption of mankind on the mountain of Golgotha, therefore, this mountain carries a spiritual significance to the believers. The writer of the Letter to the Hebrews presents a contrast between the LORD God appearing on the Mount Sinai and the Lord Jesus appearing on the mountain of Golgotha, as follows:

> Remember where you stand: not before the palpable, blazing fire of Sinai, with the darkness, gloom, whirlwind, the trumpet blast and the oracular voice, which they heard, and begged to hear no more; for they could not hear the command, 'If even an animal touches the mountain, it must be stoned.' So appalling was the sight, that Moses said, 'I shudder with fear.' No, you stand before Mount Zion and the city of the living God, heavenly

Jerusalem, before myriads of angels, the full concourse and assembly of the first-born citizens of heaven, and God the judge of all, and the spirits of good men made perfect, and Jesus the mediator of a new covenant, whose sprinkled blood has better things to tell than the blood of Abel. See that you do not refuse to hear the voice that speaks. (Heb. 12:18-22)

On the mountain of Golgotha, the glory of God's love toward mankind was manifested to save all those who would believe in the sacrifice of Jesus Christ. God in Jesus Christ is the source of our constant help. We look up to Him for help. Like the psalmist, we should say:

"I lift up my eyes to the hills of Golgotha, whence come my help. My help comes from the Lord who redeemed heaven and earth."

Recommended Hymns from the Methodist Hymnal

238 'My faith looks up to Thee,'

607 'O God of Bethel, by whose hand'

617 'Brightly gleams our banner,'

625 'I to the hills will lift mine eyes,'

Recommended Responsive Reading from the Methodist Hymnal

57 (p. 409),

Recommended Responsive Reading from *A Worship Manual for Scriptural or Methodist Order of Service*

55 (PP. 156-157).

Chapter 5

'Holiness Through Cleansing,' 'Holiness Through the Spirit of Judgment and Burning,' 'A Call to Be Holy.'

Scripture

Isaiah 4:2-6

Leviticus 11:44-45; 19:2; 20:7-8, 26

Isaiah 1: 16-18, 21-23; 2:1-5; 2:6-4:1; 6:1, 3, 5, 7; 9:1-7; 11:1-12:6; 43:6; 52:11

Hosea 1:10

Matthew 6:24; 11:28-29

Luke 16:13

John 10:10-11

II Corinthians 6:14-18; 7:1

II Timothy 2:21-22

I Peter 1:13-16

Text: Isaiah 4:4

A Few Versions of the Text, Isaiah 4:4

When the LORD shall have washed away the filth of the daughters of Zion, and purged the blood of Jerusalem from its midst, by a spirit of judgment and by a spirit of burning. *New King James Version*

when the LORD shall have washed away the filth of the daughters of Zion, and shall have purged the blood of Jerusalem from its midst thereof, by a spirit of justice, and by the spirit of burning. *The Wesleyan Bible Commentary*

when the LORD shall have washed away the filth of the daughters of Zion and cleansed the bloodstains of Jerusalem from its midst by a spirit of judgment and by a spirit of burning. *Revised Standard Version*

The LORD will wash away the filth of the women of Zion; he will cleanse the bloodstains from Jerusalem by a spirit of judgment and by a spirit of fire. *New International Version*

If the LORD washes away the filth of the women of Zion and cleanses Jerusalem from the blood that is in it by a spirit of judgment, a consuming spirit, *The New English Bible*

The LORD will wash away the filth of Zion's people. He will clean bloodstains from Jerusalem with a spirit of judgment and a spirit of burning. *God's Word*

Introduction

(1) Johann Heinrich von Dannecker (ca.1758-1841) was a German sculptor. He gained a wonderful reputation when he carved statutes of Ariadne and Greek goddesses. He was growing in his career as a sculptor. When he was at his height of the career, he thought to devote his strength and time to carve a masterpiece. He decided to carve an image of Jesus Christ. He failed twice in carving a statue of Christ. At his third attempt, he carved a perfect and beautiful image of Christ during six years, because he had a vision of Jesus Christ. Dannecker

confessed so to the people. People, who looked at the image, adored the statue of Christ.

Dannecker became so much famous that Emperor Napoleon Bonaparte (1769-1821) of the French sent for him, saying, "Come to Paris and make for me a statue of Venus for the Louvre." The offer of the French Emperor was so big that Dannecker could be tempted. Dannecker overcame the temptation; and he replied to Napoleon I, saying, "Sir, the hands that carved the Christ can never again carve a heathen goddess."[1] Or "A man who had seen Christ can never employ his gifts in carving a pagan goddess. My art is henceforth a consecrated thing."[2]

When a person is fully dedicated to God's work, it becomes impossible for him or her to do anything against the teaching of Jesus Christ. He or she cannot serve two master, as Jesus Christ said (Mt. 6:24; Lk. 16:13). He or she serves God only.

(2) King Author (ca. 460-560), the ruler of ancient Britons in the sixth century, had the Round Table of Knights. One of the knights was Sir Galahad. He was called the "Maiden Knight," because he was leading a pure life. Lord Alfred Tennyson (1809-1892), the famous poet, said about Sir Galahad: "My strength is as the strength of ten, because my heart is pure." Sir Galahad had a moral and spiritual strength. He stood firm for righteousness and justice. He did not yield to temptations; he did right things every time; therefore, all other knights used to listen to him and to respect him. In the same way, when a heart of a person is cleansed by the Holy spirit, the person gets power to resist temptations; he or she stands up and could be counted in doing right all the time.[3]

Introduction of the Text

Dannecker declined to carve a statue of a heathen goddess, because he carved a statue of Jesus Christ. While carving the statue of Jesus Christ, he was changing spiritually. He devoted himself to worship the Lord Jesus Christ; and he thought of carving a statue of a heathen goddess was against his whole hearted dedication to Jesus Christ. He did not wish to go to his former life, worshipping other gods and earning money. He wanted to remain faithful to Jesus Christ.

Like Dannecker, St. Augustine (354- 430) did not turn back to unholy and wicked life, when he devoted completely to the service of God. There are many such persons in the history of the church. How these people are made holy or saintly is told to us by the example of the people of Jerusalem, in the following words of the prophet Isaiah:

When the LORD shall have washed away the filth of the daughters of Zion and cleansed the bloodstains of Jerusalem from its midst by a spirit of judgment and by a spirit of burning. (Isaiah 4:4)

This is the text of our meditation now.

The Context of the Text

Isaiah was a prominent prophet during the times of a few kings of Judah. He was an influential advisor of the kings, a statesman, counsellor, and the prophet of the LORD God. He warned King Ahaz (735-715 B. C.) and King Hezekiah (715-687 B. C.) against trusting in foreign powers. He was at the courts of the kings of Judah until the Assyrian invasion of Judah and Jerusalem in 701 B. C. When King Sennacherib of Assyria (705-681 B. C.) invaded Judah and Jerusalem, in 701 B. C. (II Kg. 18:3), prophet Isaiah encouraged the people of Jerusalem to trust in the LORD God, who would protect them from the crisis. His encouragement to trust in God helped King Hezekiah, the inhabitants of Jerusalem, and the people of Judah. They were able to survive the Assyrian siege of 701 B. C.[4]

Prophet Isaiah watched some international events. King Tiglath-pileser III (745-727 B. C.) conquered the northern kingdom of Israel and carried many Israelites into captivity (II Kg. 15:29; I Chr. 5:26). King Shalmaneser V (727-722 B. C.) besieged Samaria for three years (724-721 B. C.) (II Kg. 17:5). Some Israelites were again carried into captivity in Assyria (II Kg. 17:6; 18:9-11). King Sennacherib (705-681 B. C.) campaigned against Judah and sieged Jerusalem in 701 B. C. Isaiah witnessed the death of King Uzziah or Azariah (783-742 B. C.), when he received his call as a prophet (Is. 6:1)

Prophet Isaiah saw the LORD God who is holy, unapproachable, majestic, and glorious. This holy God was going to restore the pride and glory of Israel, by preserving a remnant, which would be holy. Isaiah prophesied the process of cleansing the people of Judah, in these words:

> When the LORD shall have washed away the filth of the daughters of Zion and cleansed the bloodstains of Jerusalem from its midst by a spirit of judgment and by a spirit of burning. (Isaiah 4:4)

This is the text, within its historical setting.

An Analysis of the Text

This text has two ideas. (A) The first idea is that the LORD God shall have washed away the filth of the daughters of Zion and the LORD shall have cleansed the bloodstains of Jerusalem from its midst.

(B) The second idea is the means of cleansing. It is the spirit of judgment and a spirit of burning.

An Exposition of the Ideas

(A) The first idea of the text is that the LORD God shall have washed away the filth of the daughters of Zion and the LORD shall have cleansed the bloodstains of Jerusalem from its midst. This idea implies that the LORD God was going to do two acts- demolition and elevation or judgment and blessing on a grand scale on the people of Judah. These two types of actions or themes are running in the writings of prophet Isaiah, e. g. Is. 2:1-5 a vision of blessing, Is. 2:6-4:1 a judgment; Is. 9:8-21 a judgement and Is. 11:1-:12:6 a vision of blessing.[5]

God wanted to purify His people before He would accept them as His people. God is holy and pure; therefore, His people should be holy and pure. God commanded the people of Israel, saying:

> For I am the LORD your God; consecrate yourselves therefore, and be holy, for I am holy. (Lev. 11:44; cf. Lev. 11:45; 19:2; 20:7, 26).

This holiness of the people is maintained by the people by keeping His commandments. He said to them:

> Consecrate yourselves therefore, and be holy; for I am the LORD your God. Keep my statutes, and do them; I am the LORD who sanctify you. (Lev. 20:7-8)

Holiness of the people is defined as a life free from sexual adultery of any kind, a ceremonial cleanliness, and moral behaviour.

Men and women of Judah had lost holiness; they had become unholy or impure. Prophet Isaiah saw very clearly that the women and mothers of the nation are a foundation of moral character of the people. [6] When they are falling from the ethical standard, the nation as a whole cannot endure any longer. Women inculcate moral values in their children. When they are fallen, they cannot play this role effectively, because the role involves not only oral instructions but also setting a model before children. A reason of their spiritual fall was that the women of Judah had become proud of themselves. They were showing their pride and self-sufficiency through their material things and their way of walking. Prophet Isaiah wrote concerning the proudness of the women and their prideful walk, as follows:

> The LORD said: Because the daughters of Zion are haughty and walk with outstretched necks, glancing wantonly with their eyes, mincing along as they go, tinkling with their feet. (Is. 3:16)

The LORD God was displeased with the women, therefore, He was going to remove their jewellery and make them humble. Isaiah wrote about these matters in the following words:

> In that day the LORD will take way the finery of the anklets, the headbands, and the crescents; the pendants, the bracelets, the scarf; the headdresses, the armlet, the sashes, the perfume boxes, and amulets; the signet rings and nose ring; the festal robes, the mantles, the cloaks, the handbags; the garments of gauze, the linen garments, the turbans, and the veil. Instead of perfume there will be rottenness; and instead of a girdle, a rope; and instead of well-set hair, baldness; and instead of a rich robe, a girding of sackcloth; instead of beauty, shame. (Is. 3:18-24)

Like women, men of Judah had become proud because of their material prosperity. The land of Judah was filled with silver, gold, and treasures, and with horses and chariots (Is. 2:7). They were worshipping idols and consulting diviners and soothsayers (Is. 2:6, 8). The LORD God was going to bring low their haughty look and pride (Is. 2:11-12); and the men of Judah would humble before the LORD God. Because of their pride, they would be killed by the swords (Is. 3:35).

People of Jerusalem had become corrupt; they were doing injustice to one another and were not caring for widows and the orphans. Prophet Isaiah described the fallen condition of Jerusalem as follows:

> How the faithful city has become a harlot, she that was full of justice! Righteousness lodged in her, but now murderers. Your silver has become dross, your wine mixed with water. Your princes are rebels and companions of thieves. Every one loves a bribe and runs after gifts. They do not defend the fatherless, and the widow's cause does not come to them. (Is. 1: 21-24)

The LORD God, the God of justice and righteousness, was displeased with the people of Jerusalem. He was going to judge them; and purify them by the means which will be discussed shortly. He could not accept them as they were unholy and corrupt. He would make them sanctified and holy once again.

The Church, the new Israel of God, is expected to be holy and obedient, as the old Israel was. Apostle Peter exhorted Christians, saying:

> Therefore gird up your minds, be sober, set your hope fully upon the grace that is coming to you at the revelation of Jesus Christ. As obedient children, do not be conformed to the passions of your former ignorance, but as he who called you is holy, be holy yourselves in all your conduct; since it is written, 'You shall be holy, for I am holy.' (I Pet. 1:13-16)

(B) The second idea of the text is the means of cleansing. It is the spirit of judgment and a spirit of burning.

The LORD God was going to purify the people of Judah by the spirit of judgment and by the spirit of burning. These were the means God was going to purify His people and to reclaim them as His people.

How the LORD God purifies the people by a spirit of burning is given in an illustration of how Isaiah was cleansed before he became a prophet of God. Isaiah saw a vision in which he saw the LORD God sitting upon a throne and the temple was filled with His train-edge of the robe. He saw Seraphims, angels with six wings. They were covering their faces and feet. They were saying, "Holy, holy, holy, is the LORD of hosts; the whole earth is full of his glory."(Is. 6:3) When Isaiah saw the glory and holiness of God, he said:

> Woe is me! For I am lost; for I am a man of unclean lips, and I dwell in the midst of a people of unclean lips; for my eyes have seen the King, the LORD of host! (Is. 6: 5)

Then a seraphim flew to Isaiah, with a burning coal in tongs from the altar of God. The seraphim put that burning coal on the lips of Isaiah and said to him, "Behold, this has touched your lips, your guilt is taken away, and your sin is forgiven." (Is. 6:7) Isaiah was thus purified by the fire from the altar of God; and he was made consecrated vessel for God's work. He was ordained to be a prophet of God.

By the spirit of burning, the dross from the spirit of man is removed completely (Pr. 25:4). This is to be alluded that Holy Spirit is able to remove the spiritual dross from sinners; and make them just and holy for the LORD God (Jn 20:21-23; Acts 5:1-10; II Cor. 3:18; Gal. 5:22). Moreover, the spirit of burning might suggest trials and tribulation of the people, coming from the LORD God (Jas. 1:12, I Pet. 4:12-19).

The LORD God also cleanses His people by His judgment on His people. He condemns their sins and punishes them, until they realized the gravity of their sins; and turn to the LORD God for forgiveness. When He punishes the people for their iniquity, He does not want to annihilate them completely. He is gracious and forgiving God. He invites the people to be morally and spiritually clean. He offers the spirit of judgment to make them clean, with forgiveness. The LORD God spoke to the people of Judah, through prophet Isaiah, as follows:

> Wash yourselves, make yourselves clean; remove the evils of your doings from my eyes; cease to do evil, learn to do good; seek justice, correct

oppression; defend the fatherless, plead for the widow. 'Come now, let us reason together, says the LORD: though your sins are like scarlet, they shall be as white as snow; though they are red like crimson, they shall become like wool.' (Is. 1:16-18)

God in Jesus Christ invites sinners to give up their sinful life and to receive forgiveness of their sins and to get the spiritual rest. He said to the people:

Come to me, all who labour and are heavy laden, and I will give you rest. Take my yoke upon you, and learn from me; for I am gentle and lowly in heart, and you will find rest for your souls. (Mt. 11:28-29)

Jesus Christ claimed to be the door of salvation. He came into the world to give abundant life to the believers. He also claimed to be a good shepherd, giving His life for the believers. He spoke these words to the people in general:

I am the door; if any one enters by me, he will be saved, and will go in and out and find pasture. The thief comes only to steal and kill and destroy; I came that they may have life, and have it abundantly. I am the good shepherd. The good shepherd lays down his life for the sheep. (Jn 10:10-11)

Jesus Christ alone can offer forgiveness of sins to the people; and can save them for the eternal life. He also sanctifies the sinners from their spiritual filth; and set them apart from the rest of the people. The LORD God did this with the people of Israel; and He would do the same for the believers in Jesus Christ. Apostles Paul asked Christians to be separated from the unbelievers as righteousness is separated from iniquities, as light is separated from darkness, as the temple of God is separated from idols, and as Christ is separated from Belial (II Cor. 6:14-16). Then he quoted the scripture to assert the promise of God to them:

I will live in them and move among them, and I will be their God, and they shall be my people. Therefore come out from them, and be separate from them, says the Lord, and touch nothing unclean; and I will welcome you, you shall be my sons and daughters, says the Lord Almighty. (II Cor. 6:16-18 cf. Is. 52:11; 43:6; Hos. 1:10)

Then St. Paul appealed to the Christians in these words:

> Since we have these promises, beloved, let us cleanse ourselves from
> every defilement of body and spirit, and make holiness perfect in the
> fear of God. (II Cor. 7:1)

He similarly exhorted Christians to purify themselves from wickedness
and to be the vessels for the noble use in the house of the Lord, as follows:

> If any one purifies himself from what is ignoble, then he will be a vessel
> for noble use, consecrated and useful to the master of the house, ready
> for any good work. So shun youthful passions and aim at righteousness,
> faith, love, and peace, along with those who call upon the Lord from a
> pure heart. (II Tim. 2:21-22)

Jesus Christ is the saviour of all people. However, the people have a
freedom either to accept Him or reject Him as their saviour. They would
be judged on the basis of their choice. Jesus Christ said to the people:

> I have come as light into the world, that whoever believes in me may
> not remain in darkness. If any one hears my saying and does not keep
> them, I do not judge him; for I did not come to judge the world but to
> save the world. He who rejects me and does not receive my sayings has
> a judge; the word that I have spoken will be his judge on the last day.
> (Jn. 13:46-48)

Reflecting upon the judgment of the people with reference to the
incarnation of God in Jesus Christ, St. John wrote these words:

> For God so loved the world that he gave his only Son, that whoever
> believes in him should not perish but have eternal life. For God sent the
> Son into the world, not to condemn the world, but that the world might
> be saved through him. He who believes in him is not condemned; he
> who does not believe is condemned already, because he has not believed
> in the name of the only Son of God. And this is the judgment, that the
> light has come into the world, and men loved darkness rather than light,
> because their deeds were evil. (Jn 3:16-19)

In short, the people would be saved if they believe in the work and
words of Jesus Christ. This is going to be the spirit of judgment how
God would save and condemn the people.

Conclusion

When the people of God, both women and men, become unholy and corrupt, God punishes them in order to make them humble and to turn to Him for forgiveness and holiness. He provides the means of sanctifying His people. By the spirit of burning and by the spirit of judgment, God cleanses His people from all kinds of filthiness; and then He restores them as His people. He justifies sinners in the blood of Jesus Christ; He saves them by grace; and then He makes them His sons and daughters.

Recommended Hymns from the Methodist Hymnal

285 'O Breath of God, breathe on us now,'

289 'Spirit divine, attend our prayers'

300 'Breathe on me, Breath of God;'

305 'Come, Holy Ghost, our hearts inspire,'

550 'O For a heart to praise my God,'

553 'Come, Holy Ghost, all quickening fire!'

765 'Come, thou everlasting Spirt,'

779 'Come, Holy Ghost, our souls inspire,'

Recommended Responsive Reading from the Methodist Hymnal:
26 (p. 393),

Recommended Responsive Reading form *A Worship Manual for Scriptural or Methodist Order of Service*:
19 (p.102).

Endnotes

 [1] Paul Lee Tan, *Encyclopedia of 7700 Illustrations: Signs of the Times*, # 4830.

[2] *Ibid.*, # 7112.

[3] Paul Lee Tan, op. cit., # 4848.

[4] *Concise Dictionary of the Bible*, ed. Stephen Neill, John Goodwin, and Arthur Dowle, (London: Lutterworth Press, 1966), Part I, p. 155.

[5] *Asbury Bible Commentary*, ed. Eugene Carpenter and Wayne McCown, (Grand Rapids, Michigan: Zondervan Publishing House, 1992), p. 614.

[6] *The Wesleyan Bible Commentary*, (Peabody, Massachusetts: Hendrickson Publishers, 1979), Vol. III, p.28.

Chapter 6

'Redesigned for the Service of the Lord,' 'Re-moulding for Usefulness for the Lord,' 'Re-creating for Serving Divine Purpose.'

Scripture

Jeremiah 18:1-17

Genesis 12:1-3

Exodus 19:5-6; 32:9-14

Deuteronomy 7:6-11; 9:13-14, 25-29

Joshua 24:19-20, 24

Judges 2:16-19

II Chronicles 36:22-23

Ezra 1:1-4

Psalms 4:3; 107:21; 135:4

Isaiah 42:1,4,6-9; 64:6-11

Ezekiel 33:10-11

Hosea 5:14-6:2

Joel 2:12-13

Acts 9:15

Romans 8:28-30

Text: Jeremiah 18:4

A Few Versions of the Text, Jeremiah 18:4

And the vessel that he made of clay was marred in the hand of the potter; so he made it again into another vessel, as it seemed good to the potter to make. *New King James Version*

And when the vessel that he made of the clay was marred in the hand of the potter, he made it again another vessel, as seemed good to the potter to make it. *The Wesleyan Bible Commentary*

The vessel he was making of clay was spoiled in the potter's hand, and he reworked it into another vessel, as it seemed good to the potter to do. *Revised Standard Version*

But the pot he was shaping from the clay was marred in his hands; so the potter formed it into another pot, shaping it as seemed best to him. *New International Version*

Now and then a vessel he was making out of the clay would be spoilt in his hands, and then he would start again and mould it into another vessel to his liking. *The New English Bible*

But the jar that he was forming didn't turn out as he wished, so he kneaded it into a lump and started again. *The Living Bible Illustrated*

Whenever a clay pot he was working on was ruined, he would rework it into a new clay pot the way he wanted to make it. *God's Word*

Introduction

(1) After 1980 Canadian economy began to see the adverse effects of recession. The Canadian government and private sectors began to cut down the cost of their management; they were reducing their employees and reducing their services. During such a critical time, a company was building a large building for its offices. The company built four storey building, which would have cost a few millions dollars. The building is in Burlington, beside the Q. E. W. high way. After building four storey building, the company decided to demolish the structure and to re-build it.

When the company demolished the structure, I felt it was a huge waste of money and material. The company decided to demolish the structure, because the structure was not going to serve the purpose of the company adequately. The company was ready to bear the loss in order to have a better structure, serving the purpose of the company.

(2) We always see old firms going out of business and new firms coming into existence. Whenever a new business in opened in a mall, that particular part of the mall gets re-designed or re-modelled, in order to serve the purpose of the new business. All businesses have different purposes, therefore, they require different setups. As they require different designs, redesigning sections of the mall becomes an ongoing concern.

Introduction of the Text

The purpose of business people calls for the changes in structure. This principle seems to apply to our social and religious life. God is our creator and designer. He has purposes in His mind whenever He acts in our national history. God, through prophet Jeremiah, spoke about this principle, in the following words:

> **The vessel he was making of clay was spoiled in the potter's hand, and he reworked it into another vessel, as it seemed good to the potter to do. (Jeremiah 18:4)**

This is the text of our meditation now.

The Context of the Text

Prophet Jeremiah spoke these words of the text to the people of Israel. He told them that the LORD God asked Jeremiah to go to the potter's house in order to give him an object lesson or message through an acted parable to the people of Israel.

When prophet Jeremiah went to the potter's house, he saw the potter working at his wheel. He saw a vessel, which the potter was making out of the clay, spoiled in the potter's hand. The potter did not throw away the spoiled vessel. He kept the spoiled vessel on the wheel; he crushed and squeezed the wrong shape of the spoiled vessel; he made it again a clay without shape and then reworked into another vessel. He gave a different shape as seemed good to the potter.

An Analysis of the Text

This text has two spiritual ideas. (A) The first idea is that the vessel, which the potter was intending to make out of the clay, was spoiled in his hand.

(B) The second idea is that the potter reworked on the clay to make it into another vessel, as it seemed good to him.

An Exposition of the Textual Ideas

(A) The first idea is that the vessel, which the potter was intending to make out of the clay, was spoiled in his hand. The potter had a purpose in his mind before he started to work on the clay. As he was making a vessel, according to his purpose, the vessel was spoiled in his hand. The cause of spoiling the vessel was not the potter; it was not a fault of the potter that the vessel was spoiled in his hand. The cause of spoiling the vessel was in the clay. There was a small stone or a piece of sand in the clay. Therefore, the clay was not so soft to yield to the gentle pressure which was applied by the potter in order to make a vessel.

This illustration is applied to the people of God. God chose the people of Israel to be His people. He had a purpose for which He chose them as His people. The purpose of the election of the people of Israel is traced back to Abram. God chose Abram out of his tribe and asked him to leave his people and the land and to go to the promised land and to inherit it for his descendants. God made a covenant with Abram, saying:

> Go from your country and your kindred and your father's house to the land that I will show you. And I will make of you a great nation, and I will bless you, and make your name great, so that you will be a blessing. I will bless those who bless you, and him who curses you I will curse; and by you all the families of the earth shall bless themselves. (Gen. 12:1-3)

These verses tell us that God chose Abram to be a father of the nation of Israel; he and his descendants would be a blessing to other nations. This was the original purpose why God chose Abram. God changed Abram's name into Abraham, when Abram was ninety-nine years old and God made a covenant with him (Gen. 17:1-8).

God kept His promise, which He gave to Abraham, Isaac, and Jacob, by liberating the people of Israel out of the bondage of the Egyptians, through Moses. Moses led the people through wilderness to see the promised land. After redeeming the people from the slavery of Pharaoh, Moses reminded them of the purpose of God in electing them as His own possession, because of His love toward them. He said:

> For you are a people holy to the LORD your God; the LORD your God has chosen you to be a people for his own possession, out of all the peoples that are on the face of the earth. It was not because you were more in number than any other people that the LORD set his love upon you and chose you, for you were the fewest of all peoples; but it is because the LORD loves you, and is keeping the oath which he swore to your fathers, that the LORD has brought you out with a mighty hand, and redeemed you from the house of bondage, from the the hand of Pharaoh king of Egypt. Know therefore that the LORD your God is God, the faithful God who keeps covenant and steadfast love with those who love him and keep his commandments, to a thousand generations, and requites to their face those who hate him, by destroying them; he will not be slack with him who hates him, and he will requite him to his face. You shall therefore be careful to do the commandments, and the statutes, and the ordinances, which I command you this day. (Deut. 7:6-11)

These words of exhortation refer to God's purpose of choosing the people of Israel as His own people. They were to be a treasured possession of God (Ps. 135:4); they were to be godly people (Ps. 4:3). They were expected to love the LORD God by being obedient to His commandments and the statutes. They were to be holy by keeping God's righteous commandments (Deut.7:11). God's commandments were for justice and righteousness, to be kept among His people. God's chosen people had to stand by those ethical virtues. They would become a blessing to other nations, when they would abide by these virtues. These are the purposes why God chose Israel to be His godly and holy people.

God had these purposes to mould the social, moral, and political life of the people of Israel. But the people of Israel did not obey the commandments of God. They became worshippers of other gods. They became morally corrupt.

They were engaged in all kinds of sins. They perpetuated the moral and spiritual corruption by their stubbornness.

As sand or a small stone hardens clay, a potter cannot make a vessel out of such clay. The potter has to remove the hardness from the clay by taking away the small stone. Otherwise, he would be unable to make a vessel out of the clay. This principle was to be applied to the life of the chosen people of God. A nation is like a clay in the hand of God. He has the sovereign authority on the life of the people. His authority cannot be challenged by anyone.

Clay becomes hard by the presence of sand or small stone in the clay. In a similar way, the stubbornness of the people makes them so hard that they cannot be moulded for the divine purpose. A history of the people of Israel cites many occasions when they rebelled against God. Let us refer to a few occasions.

(1) God called Moses to meet Him on the mount to receive the ten commandments. Moses was delayed to come down from the mountain. The people of Israel put public pressure on Aaron to make gods for them. Aaron asked them to bring gold and he made a molten calf for them; he built an altar to sacrifice to the golden calf. They worshipped the golden calf and honoured it as a god; they ascribed their god the honour and praise saying it brought them out of the Egyptian bondage. God was angry with the people of Israel, because they worshipped an idol and gave it His honour and power. In His anger He said to Moses:

> I have seen this people, and behold, it is a stiff-necked people; now
> therefore let me alone, that my wrath may burn hot against them and I
> may consume them; but of you I will make a great nation. (Ex. 32:9-10;
> Deut. 9:13-14)

Then Moses pleaded to God not to destroy the people of Israel whom
He liberated (Ex. 32:11-14; Deut. 9:25-29). God changed His mind and
spared the people from destruction.

(2) After Moses, Joshua became the leader of the people of Israel.
He won battles against the people, who were residing in the promised
land. He established the people of Israel as a nation amidst other people-
Canaanites, Jebusite, Amorites, Philistines, etc. Joshua perceived a
possibility that the people of Israel would forget and forsake the LORD
God and serve other gods. Therefore, he warned them, saying:

> You cannot serve the LORD; for he is a holy God; he is a jealous God;
> he will not forgive your transgressions or your sins. If you forsake the
> LORD and serve foreign gods, then he will turn and do you harm, and
> consume you, after having done you good. (Jos. 24:19-20)

Then the people made a covenant to serve the LORD God only and to
be faithful to Him (Jos. 24:24).

(3) After the death of Joshua, the people began to worship other
gods. They angered the LORD God by worshipping other gods.
God punished them for their disobedience and sins. God allowed the
rulers of other races to subdue Israel and treat them with harshness.
When the people of Israel cried to the LORD to deliver them from
oppression, God raised judges for them and gave them rest from time
to time. When the judges died, they turned to other gods and they did
not drop any of their evil practices or their stubborn ways. (Jud. 2:16-19)

(4) The stubborn ways of worshipping other gods were continued
by the kings and the people of Israel when there were two kingdoms
of Israel. God punished them for their sins by sending them into exile.
(II Kg. 17:23; 24:14-16)

(B) The second idea is that the potter reworked on the clay to make it into another vessel, as it seemed good to him. When the potter saw the vessel being spoiled in his hand because of a stone in the clay, he had two choices of actions, namely, either to throw away the whole clay or to remove the stone from the clay and make another vessel. The potter, whom prophet Jeremiah went to see, chose a second alternative, i.e., to rework the clay into another vessel, as it seemed good to him. This acted parable was applied to the life of the people of Israel.

The LORD God did not abandon His chosen people instantly, when they acted rebelliously or stubbornly; but He showed patience toward them always. He punished them several times. But He did not destroy them in His wrath. God is always merciful and full of compassion. His purpose of punishing His people was to correct them and to make them faithful and righteous people. God sent this message through His servants, the prophets.

God through prophet Ezekiel declared His intention to the people of Israel as to why He was punishing them. He appealed them, saying:

> Thus have you said: 'Our transgressions and our sins are upon us, and we waste away because of them; how then can we live?' Say to them, As I live, says the LORD God, I have no pleasure in the death of the wicked, but that the wicked turn from his way and live; turn back, turn back from your evil ways. (Ezek. 33:10-11)

How God punishes and shows His mercy to the repentant was explained by Him through prophet Hosea, in the following words:

> For I will be like a lion to Ephraim, and like a young lion to the house of Judah. I, even I, will rend and go away, I will carry off, and none shall rescue. I will return again to my place, until they acknowledge their guilt and seek my face, and in their distress they seek me, saying, 'Come, let us return to the LORD God; for he has torn, that he may heal us; he has stricken, and he will bind us up. After two days he will revive us; on the third day he will raise us up, that we may live before him. (Hos. 5:14-6:2)

God sent the similar message through prophet Joel, as follows:

> Yet even now, says the LORD, return to me with all your heart, with fasting, with weeping, and with mourning; and rend your hearts and not

> your garments. Return to the LORD, your God, for he is gracious and merciful, slow to anger, and abounding in steadfast love, and repents of evil. (Joel 2:12-13)

On behalf of the people of Israel, prophet Isaiah confessed their sins and asked for God's mercy, in the following words:

> We have all become like one who is unclean, and all our righteous deeds are like a polluted garment. We all fade like a leaf, and our iniquities, like the wind, takes away. There is no one that calls upon thy name, that bestirs himself to take hold of thee, for thou hast hid thy face from us, and has delivered us into the hand of our iniquities. Yet, O LORD, thou art our Father; we are the clay, and thou art our potter; we are all the work of thy hand. Be not exceedingly angry, O LORD, and remember not iniquity for ever. Behold, consider, we are all thy people. Thy holy cities have become a wilderness, Jerusalem a desolation. Our holy and beautiful house, where our fathers praised thee, has been burned by fire, and all our pleasant places have become ruins. (Is. 64:6-11)

God heard the cry of His people and He made king Cyrus (539-530 B. C.) of Persia to issue the decree of return of the Jews to Judah and Jerusalem to rebuild the temple and the walls of Jerusalem (II Chr. 36:22-23; Ezra 1:1-4) in ca. 538 B. C. God brought them back to their promised land once again.

The return of the exiles to the promised land indicated how the LORD God dealt with the people of Israel mercifully, when they repented of their sins and turned to Him. He gave them another opportunity to serve Him and to be His people once again. This divine act is similar to the act of the potter who reworked the clay into another vessel, as it seemed good to him. The LORD God redesigned the people of Israel to serve His purposes, which are mentioned above.

The people of Israel as a whole were not faithful to the LORD God in fulfilling His purposes, behind their choice. They did not become the instrument of blessing for other nations. Therefore, the prophets were looking forward to the Messiah, in whom the divine purposes would be fulfilled. Prophet Isaiah prophesied about the Messiah, the chosen servant of God, in the following words:

> Behold my servant, whom I uphold, my chosen, in whom my soul delights; I have put my Spirit upon him, he will bring forth justice to the nations..... He will not fail or be discouraged till he has established justice in the earth; and the coastlands wait for his law.... 'I am the LORD, I have called you in righteousness, I have taken you by the hand and kept you; I have given as a covenant to the people, a light to the nations, to open the eyes that are blind, to bring out the prisoners from the dungeon, from the prison those who sit in darkness. I am the LORD, that is my name; my glory I give to no other, nor my praise to graven images. Behold, the former things have come to pass, and new things I now declare; before they spring forth I tell you of them. (Is. 42:1, 4, 6-9)

Jesus Christ the Messiah fulfilled the purpose of God. He came into the world to establish the universal church, the new Israel. Christians are now the true Israel, a chosen race, a royal priesthood, a holy nation (I Pet. 2:9). The purpose of their divine election is made clear to them. They have to declare the wonderful deeds of Him who called them out of darkness (I Pet. 2:9 cf. Ex. 19:5-6; Ps. 107:21). They have to proclaim the gospel of the Lord Jesus, as St. Paul did (Acts 9:15). They have to bear witness to others, how they are saved by His grace. God is not going to allow His good purposes to fail, but He will fulfil them through His chosen people, the universal Church (Rom. 8:28-30).

Conclusion

Believers in Jesus Christ are chosen people of the LORD God. They have to repent of their sins and stubbornness before Him and allow Him to reshape them, according to His divine purposes. They have to be new creation (II Cor. 5:17) in order to fulfill their calling. Let those divine purposes be fulfilled through His true new Israel, the universal Church.

Recommended Hymns from the Methodist Hymnal

300 'Breathe on me, Breath of God;'

448 'O Love that will not let me go,'

611 'Lead us, heavenly Father, lead us'

Recommended Hymns from Sacred Songs and Solos
122 'Have thine own way'

608 'Take time to be holy'

Recommended Responsive Readings from the Methodist Hymnal
53 (p. 407),

Recommended Responsive Reading from *A Worship Manual for Scriptural or Methodist Order of Service*
50 (pp. 148-149).

Chapter 7

'Jesus Christ's Prayer in the Gethsemane,'
'Prayerful Loneliness with God,'
'Watch and Pray Before Temptation Arrives,'
'Keep awake and Pray before Crises.'

Scripture

Matthew 26:36-44

Genesis 21:15-17

II Kings 19:10-12, 15-19, 35-37; 20:2-3, 5-6

Psalms 22:1; 107:27-28; 142:1-2

Zechariah 13:7

Matthew 4:11; 17:1-7; 26:2, 21-25, 31-35, 41-44, 47, 52-54, 66-68; 27:28-31, 39-44

Mark 1:35; 14:32-42

Luke 6:12-13; 22:39-46

Hebrews 5:7-9

Text: Matthew 26:38

A Few Versions of the Text, Matthew 26:38

Then he said to them, "My soul is exceedingly sorrowful, even to death. Stay here and watch with me." *New King James Version*

Then saith he to them, My soul is exceedingly sorrowful, even unto death: tarry ye here, and watch with me. *Explanatory Notes Upon the New Testament*

Then he said to them, "My soul is very sorrowful, even to death. Remain here and watch with me." *Revised Standard Version*

Then he said to them, "My soul is overwhelmed with sorrow to the point of death. Stay here and keep watch with me." *New International Version*

and he said to them, 'My heart is ready to break with grief. Stop here, and stay awake with me.' *The New English Bible*

Then he told them, "My soul is crushed with horror and sadness to the point of death...stay here...stay awake with me." *The living Bible Illustrated*

Then he said to them, "My anguish is so great that I feel as if I'm dying. Wait here, and stay awake with me." *God's Word*

Introduction

When the believers pray to God very earnestly in the time of crises, God hears them and delivers them from dangers; and He gives them strength to bear the strain of the calamities. When Martin Rinkart (A. D. 1586 -1649) and his people were relieved out of such sever hardship, he wrote the following hymn:

Now thank we all our God

With hearts and hands and voices,

Who wondrous things hath done,

In who His world rejoices;

Who from our mothers' arms

Hath blessed us on our way

with countless gifts of love,

And still is ours today.

O may this bounteous God

Thru all our life be near us,

With ever joyful hearts

And blessed peace to cheer us,

And keep us in His grace,

And guide us when perplexed,

And free us from all ills

In this world and the next.

Martin Rinkart (A. D. 1586-1649) was born in Eilenberg, Saxony, Germany. At the age of thirty-one, he was called to be the pastor of the Lutheran Church in his native town. He arrived in Eilenberg when a bloodshed started. The wars lasted thirty years (1618-1648). Eilenberg was a walled city; therefore, it became crowded with political refugees and military fugitives. During those war years, several pestilence and famines arose; various armies marched through the town, leaving death and destruction. The town was invaded once by Austrian army, and twice by the Swedish army.

During an occupation by the Swedish army, the impoverished town was asked to make a large tribute payment. Rinkart interceded with the leaders of the army to reduce the tribute; but the Swedish commander would not at first consider Rinkart's request. Then the pastor turned to his parishioners and said, "Come, my children, we can find no mercy with man; let us take refuge with God." The pastor and the people were praying and singing hymns. Their demonstration of spiritual fervency moved the Swedish commander; and he finally lowered the tribute payment.

The second verse of the hymn is a petition for God's continued care and keeping; and it hints at Rinkart's personal hardship.[1] God delivered Rinkart and the people from crises. This had been the experience of many devout persons that God delivers believers from the crises when they earnestly cry for His help and guidance.

Introduction of the Text

When we reflect on the teaching and healing ministry of Jesus Christ, we would know that he was a man of prayer. He prayed to God for His help and guidance. He had a habit to rise up early in the morning, before daybreak and to go out in a lonely place to pray to God, leaving his disciples behind (Mk 1:35; Lk. 4:42). He went out to the mountain and prayed all night, seeking God's guidance and approval before he chose his twelve disciples whom he named apostles (Lk. 6:12-13). He wished to be alone with God, seeking His guidance. God guided Jesus Christ throughout his ministry and made his ministry a success.

When Jesus knew that the hour of his being crucified was approaching, his heart was filled with heavy sorrow. He took his disciples to Gethsemane garden. He left his eight disciples at the grove of the garden and took his three intimate disciples with him. He wished to be alone with God; therefore, he wanted to leave them behind. Before he left them, he acted in this way:

> Then he said to them, "My soul is very sorrowful, even to death. Remain here and watch with me." (Matthew 26:38)

This is the text of our meditation now.

The Context of the Text

Jesus Christ and his eleven disciples went in the Gethsemane garden in order to prepare themselves to face the forthcoming calamities. Jesus Christ was filled with sorrow due to many reasons. He wanted to prepare himself to accept his agonizing death on a cross. He wanted to pray to God for strength to face the calamity.

When Jesus and his eleven disciples entered the grove of Gethsemane, he said to his disciples, 'Sit here, while I go yonder and pray.' (Mt. 26:36) Having said so, he took with him Peter, James and John, the two sons of Zebedee, who were his intimate disciples, leaving other eight disciples at the grove. Having gone further with those three disciples, he said to them:

> My soul is very sorrowful, even to death. Remain here and watch with me.
> (Matthew 26:38)

This is the text, within its historical background.

An Analysis of the Text

This text has two ideas. (A) The first idea is that the soul of Jesus Christ was very sorrowful, even to death.

(B) The second idea is that Jesus Christ asked his intimate disciples to remain here [i.e., at the closest distance] and watch with him.

An Exposition of the Textual Ideas

(A) The first idea is that the soul of Jesus Christ was very sorrowful, even to death. We should know the reasons why Jesus Christ was filled with intensive sorrow. (1) Jesus Christ had a prophetic power to know the events in advance. He knew that those events were sorrowful; therefore, his soul or heart was filled with agony. He prophesied to his disciples, "You know that after two days the Passover is coming, and the Son of man will be delivered up to be crucified." (Mt. 26:2) In other words, Jesus Christ knew that he would be nailed to the cross. He knew the manner of his death. It was going to be a humiliating death for him. He prophesied the mode of his death two days before the Passover Feast.

(2) When Jesus and his disciples had a Passover Feast, he said to them, during the celebration of the feast: "Truly, I say to you, one of you will betray me." (Mt. 26:21) The disciples were upset and they began to ask Jesus, one after another, saying, "Is it I, Lord." (Mt.26:22) Then Jesus specifically answered them, saying, "He who has dipped his hand in the dish with me, will betray me." (Mt.26:23) When Judas asked Jesus

the same question, saying, "Is it I, Master?" (Mt. 26:25) Jesus answered him, saying, "You have said so." (Mt. 26:25) Dipping bread in a dish is an oriental way of expressing one's intimate friendship and loyalty. Jesus told his disciples that the one who showed himself intimately friendly and trustworthy would betray him. Jesus knew beforehand that Judas Iscariot would betray him.

(3) After their Passover Feast, Jesus Christ said to his disciples, prophesying, "You will all fall away because of me this night; for it is written, 'I will strike the shepherd, and the sheep of the flock will be scattered.'" (Mt.26:31) This was prophesied by prophet Zechariah (Zec. 13:7). Then Peter wanted to assure Jesus his personal and exclusive loyalty, saying, "Though they all fall away because of you, I will never fall away." (Mt.26:33) Then Jesus answered to Peter, saying: "Truly, I say to you, this very night, before the cock crows, you will deny me three times." (Mt.26:34) Peter and other ten disciples assured Jesus that they would not say that they never knew Jesus, even though they have to die with him. (Mt. 26:35) They tried to comfort him by assuring their loyalty and friendship to him, even at the cost of their life. But Jesus knew that they would desert him, as the scripture has foretold. Their abandonment of him made him sorrowful.

(4) Jesus Christ knew how the people would treat him; they would lay false charges against him (Mt. 26:61). He would be denied justice and fairness during his trial (Mt. 26:59-60). He would be condemned to death (Mt. 26:66). Some people would spit in his face and would strike in his face and on the body (Mt. 26:67-68). The soldiers would ridicule him (Mt. 27:28-29); they would strike him and nailed him to a cross (Mt. 27:30-31). Some people would ridicule him while he would be on the cross (Mt. 27:39-44). This kind of treatment made him sorrowful.

(5) Jesus Christ knew that as he was carrying the sins of the world on his head, even God would forsake him for some time. Jesus knew about this prophecy (Ps. 22:1). This temporary abandonment of God made Jesus sorrowful.

For these reasons, the soul or heart of Jesus Christ was filled with grave sorrow. His sorrow was so great that he felt he would die by the burden of his sorrow.

(B) The second idea of the text is that Jesus Christ asked his intimate disciples to remain here [i.e., at the closest distance] and watch with him. Jesus Christ said these words to his intimate disciples. The intimacy between Jesus and his three disciples was evident when he took them on a mountain where he was transfigured in their presence (Mt. 17:1-7). Jesus gave them a special privilege of his manifestation as the Son of God. These three disciples formed an inner circle of Jesus' disciples. When his heart was filled with immense sorrow, he took them with him, leaving other eight disciples at the grove of the garden.

Jesus Christ wanted to be alone, expressing his burden of anxiety to God. Therefore, he left his intimate disciples behind him and went a little farther from them to pray. He asked them to stay behind and watch with him.

Jesus Christ did not ask his intimate disciples to pray with him or to share his personal burden with them. His burden was so heavy that he could not and did not share it with them. He alone had to carry the burden, i.e., the burden of the sins of the world. Others were not commissioned to share this special burden with him. Jesus Christ was chosen to be the sinless Lamb of God to offer his blood for the forgiveness of the world.

Jesus Christ asked his closest disciples to stay behind and watch with him. He went a little farther from them and prayed to God with whole of his being. He said to God:

"My Father, if it be possible, let this cup pass from me; nevertheless, not as I will, but as thou wilt." (Mt. 26:39)

St. Luke rendered the saying of Jesus, in these words: "Father, if thou art willing, remove this cup from me; nevertheless not my will, but thine, be done." (Lk. 22:42) Jesus prayed to God to take away the cup of sufferings from him, if it was the will of God. The cup of sufferings included humiliation by the people, injustice done by a religious council, ridicule of the soldiers and of the people, physical torture on the cross, rejection of his disciples, and abandonment of God. This cup of agony was heavy for Jesus Christ. He wished that the cup be removed from him. However, he fully submitted to the sovereign will of God and asked God to remove the cup if it was His will. This prayer of Jesus demonstrated his utter unselfishness and unreserved submission to the will of God.

Jesus Christ had asked his three disciples to watch with him when he went a little farther from them to pray.

He came back and found his disciples sleeping. Peter was somewhat awake. Jesus said to him, "So could you not watch [or keep awake] with me one hour? Watch and pray that you may not enter into temptation; the spirit is willing, but the flesh is weak." (Mt. 26:41) Peter and other two disciples- John and James, sons of Zebedee- were not able to keep themselves awake, because they were tired. Jesus exhorted Peter to keep awake and pray so that he might not enter into temptation. The temptation of the disciples was to depend on their strength rather than to depend on God for His strength. Jesus went away from his disciples second time and prayed, "My Father, if this cannot pass unless I drink, thy will be done." (Mt.26: 42) Jesus came back and found them sleeping, because their eyes were heavy. He again went a third time to pray and said the same words in his prayer. (Mt. 26:44) The way how Jesus prayed in agony and how God responded to his prayer is stated in the Gospel according to St. Luke, in these words:

> And there appeared to him an angel from heaven, strengthening him. And being in agony he prayed more earnestly; and his sweat became like great drops of blood falling down upon the ground. (Lk. 22:43-44)

This event should remind us of a similar event when Jesus was strengthened by an angel of the LORD God (Mt. 4:11), after the Evil One left Jesus Christ testing.

Reflecting on the earthly life of Jesus Christ, the writer of the Letter to the Hebrews wrote about his prayerful life and God's response to his earnest prayer, in these words:

> In the days of his flesh, Jesus offered up prayers and supplications, with loud cries and tears, to him who was able to save him from death, and he was heard for his godly fear. Although he was a Son, he learned obedience through what he suffered; and being made perfect he became the source
> of eternal salvation to all who obey him,.. (Heb. 5:7-9)

There are a few events in the Bible to illustrate the point how God answered the prayers of those who prayed to the LORD God earnestly and in agony. Let us find those events and individuals.

(1) Hagar and her son Ishmael were wandering in the wilderness of Beer-sheba. The water in the skin was gone. The child was thirsty and about to die of thirst. The child lifted its voice and wept. The LORD God heard the cry of the child. The angel of the LORD God said to Hagar:

> What troubles you, Hagar? Fear not; for God has heard the voice of the lad where he is. Arise, lift up the lad, and hold him fast with your hand; for I will make him a great nation. (Gen. 21:17-18)

God heard the cry of Ishmael and He knew the anxiety of Hagar and He answered them by providing water and by promising them to make a great nation of Ishmael.

(2) Sennacherib (705-681 B. C.), king of Assyria, wrote a letter to Hezekiah (715-687 B. C.), king of Judah, threatening him to submit and not to trust in his God, as follows:

> Do not let your God on whom you rely deceive you by promising that Jerusalem will not be given into the hand of the king of Assyria. Behold, you have heard what the kings of Assyria have done to all lands, destroying them utterly. And shall you be delivered? Have the gods of the nations delivered them, the nations which my fathers destroyed, Gozan, Haran, Rezeph, and the people of Eden who were in Telassar ?.. (II Kg. 19:10-12)

King Hezekiah read the letter and he went to the temple of the LORD God; he prayed earnestly to God to save Jerusalem and his kingdom (II Kg. 19:15-19). Then God sent prophet Isaiah with the message of assurance of protecting Jerusalem (II Kg. 19:22-34). God sent His angel, who slew 185,000 soldiers of Sennacherib. Sennacherib returned to Nineveh; and his son killed him in a temple. (II Kg. 19:35-37)

(3) King Hezekiah (715-687 B. C.) became sick and was at the point of death. Prophet Isaiah went to see him and told him the message of God to set his house in order; and he would die. Then the king prayed to the LORD earnestly and asked God to remember the good deeds he performed. He wept bitterly in his prayer (II Kg. 20:2-3). God heard his prayer and saw his tears; and sent Isaiah back to the king with the message that God would heal him on the third day and add fifteen years to his life; and He would deliver Jerusalem from the hand of the king of Assyria (II Kg. 20:5-6).

(4) A psalm writer generalized these events and wrote that the LORD God hears the cry of the afflicted people; and He delivers them from their distress. (Ps. 107:26-32 cf. Ps. 142:1-2)

God answered the prayer of Jesus Christ, His Son by giving him the divine strength. Then Jesus Christ went back to his three disciples and asked them to rise and to keep going, because his betrayer was approaching near. While Jesus was speaking to them, Judah Iscariot led the crowd to arrest Jesus (Mt. 26:47).

The three disciples could not keep themselves awake; they were fast asleep; therefore, they were not praying to God, seeking His guidance and strength in the time of crisis.

Instead of depending on God, they depended upon their strength. One of them resorted to violence. Jesus rebuked the disciple who used his sword in the crisis. The disciples did not realize that the arrest of Jesus was in accordance with will of God; and in accordance with the scriptures (Mt. 26:52-54). Jesus fully depended on God and he overcame the temptation. But his disciples depended on their own strength in the time of crises and they failed.

Conclusion

When the heart of Jesus Christ was filled with intense sorrows, resulting from - betrayal of Judas Iscariot, rejection of his other disciples, a temporary abandonment by God, false charges of the few persons, denial of justice by the religious and secular authority, humiliation by the soldiers, and cruel death on the cross. He wanted to pray earnestly to God for His guidance and help. He fully submitted to the will of God. Because of his obedience, God raised him from the dead. The believers should pray to God in a solitary place; they should submit to His will. Then God will make them successful.

Recommended Hymns from the Methodist Hymnal

165 'Forty days and forty nights'

168 'Lord! it is good for us to be'

493 'Love of love, and Light of light,'

586 'Stay, Master, stay upon this heavenly hill.'

Recommended Responsive Reading from the Methodist Hymnal

41 (p. 401) or

69 (p. 414),

Recommended Responsive Readings from *A Worship Manual for Scriptural or Methodist Order of Service*

35 (pp. 125-127) or

68 (pp. 174-175).

Chapter 8

'The Trial of Jesus Christ,'
'Injustice to the Saviour of the World,'
'Conspiracy Against the Christ,'
'Conspiracy of the Religious Body Against Jesus Christ,'
'Mockery of Justice by a Religious Crowd.'

Scripture

Matthew 26:57-27:1-26

Isaiah 53:3-7

Matthew 6:2-6; 9:10-13; 12:10-14; 15:3-9, 12; 21:13, 23;
26:3-4, 6-15, 47-48; 27:17, 20, 22-26

Mark 3:1-6; 14:1-9

Luke 13:10-17; 14:1-4;19:48; 22:39, 47, 54; 23:2-7, 10-11, 14-16

John 12:1-6; 18:2-3

I Corinthians 15:3-4

I Peter 2:22-25

Text: Matthew 26:66

A Few Versions of the Text, Matthew 26:66
'What do you think?' They answered and said, 'He is deserving of death.'
New King James Version

What think ye? They answering and said, 'He is worthy of death.'
Explanatory Notes Upon the New Testament

"What is your judgment?" They answered, "He deserves death."
Revised Standard Version

'What do you think?' "He is worthy of death," they answered.
New International Version

'What is your opinion?' 'He is guilty,' they answered; 'he should die.' *The New English Bible*

"What is your verdict?" They shouted, "Death! -Death! -Death!"
The Living Bible Illustrated

"What's your verdict?" They answered "He deserves the death penalty!" *God's Word*

Introduction
Lenten Season is a very special season for Christians, because it reminds them of what the Lord Jesus Christ said and did during the last days of his earthly ministry. Lenten Season begins with Ash Wednesday. Most preachers prepare believers for a closer fellowship with God by preaching on a theme of repentance and restoration of fellowship with God. The Holy Week is the last part of the Lenten Season. The Holy Week or the Passion Week begins on Palm Sunday. Preachers preach sermons on the triumphal entry of the Lord Jesus Christ in Jerusalem. After this Sunday, preachers preach on the event of Jesus purifying the temple, on other events, and the last Passover feast of Jesus Christ with his disciples. Then comes the Good Friday. Preachers preach on the seven words or utterances which Jesus said from the cross. The Lenten Season

is concluded with Easter Sunday, the day when Jesus Christ rose from the dead; and became victorious over death and sin. Preachers preach on the importance of the resurrection of the Lord Jesus Christ and its implications for and application to the life of the believers.

Preachers in general follow the pattern of preaching sermons during the Lenten Season. However, many of the preachers lose the sight of the trial of Jesus Christ; and they do not preach on the trial of Jesus Christ. Therefore, we should think of this matter, which is generally overlooked.

Introduction of the Text

The trial of Jesus Christ is very important for believers for various reasons. From a judicial point of view, we have to examine whether Jesus Christ was legally and properly treated by the authorities, which were supposed to uphold the law of the LORD God and of the land.

We should note that the people, who were hired by the religious council of Jews to conspire against Jesus Christ, shouted, "he deserves death," during the process of the trial of Jesus Christ. They shouted this before the high priest, who initiated the trial, and before Pontius Pilate, the Governor of Judea, who concluded the trial.

The crowd shouted, "he [Jesus] deserves death," (Matthew 26: 66)

This is the text of our meditation now.

The Context of the Text

Two days before the Passover feast and the feast of Unleavened Bread, the chief priests and the scribes were seeking to arrest Jesus and to kill him (Mt. 26:3-4; Mk 14:1-2). They were looking for someone to help them arrest Jesus, after the feast because they were afraid of the people, revolting against them. Jesus and his disciples used to go to the temple in Jerusalem; but no one dared to arrest Jesus (Mt.26:55), because people believed Jesus to be a prophet of God (Lk. 19:48).

Jesus and his disciples were at Bethany in the house of Simon the leper. A woman went there; and anointed Jesus with an expensive ointment (Mt. 26:6-13; Mk 14:3-9 cf. Jn 12:1-3). Judas Iscariot objected against the act of the woman, saying it was a waste of money (Jn 12:4-6). He was the treasurer of the group.

Judas Iscariot went to the chief priests and said to them, "What will you give me if I deliver him [Jesus] to you?" They paid him thirty pieces of silver. From that moment, Judas began to seek an opportunity to betray Jesus (Mt. 26:14-15).

It was a custom of Jesus Christ to go to the Mount of Olives to pray at night (Lk. 22:39). His eleven disciples followed him to Gethsemane Garden at night, after they had the Passover feast. Judas Iscariot, one of the disciples of Jesus Christ, had left Jesus and other disciples at the beginning of their Passover feast; he was not with the group. He went to Sanhedrin, the Council of the Jews, to tell them how to execute the arrest of Jesus, for which he was paid money in advance.

Judas led a great crowd with swords and clubs, from the chief priests and the elders of the Jewish council (Mt. 26:47; Lk. 22:47), to the garden of Gethsemane, where Jesus and his eleven disciples used to go at night (Lk. 22:39; Jn 18:2-3). Judas had told the crowd that he would kiss Jesus as a sign to identify Jesus; and the crowd should arrest Jesus (Mt. 26:48). When Judas kissed Jesus, the crowd arrested Jesus.

The crowd arrested Jesus; and took him to the house of the high priest (Lk. 22:54), Caiphas, where the scribes and elders had gathered (Mt. 26:57). It was a gathering of the council, held at down. The council sought false charges against Jesus that they might put him to death; but they found none (Mt. 26:59-60). Then the high priest put Jesus under solemn oath; and asked him to tell them if he was the Christ, the Son of God (Mt. 26:63). Jesus gave him an ambiguous reply. Then the high priest tore his robe; and accused Jesus of blasphemy. Then he asked the crowd, saying, "What is your judgment?" The crowd replied, "He deserves death." (Mt. 26:66) This is the text of our meditation, within its historical setting.

An Analysis of the Text

This text has two ideas. (A) The first idea is the question of the high priest, Caiphas, to the crowd, "What is your judgment?"

(B) The second idea is the answer of the crowd saying, "He deserves death."

An Exposition of the Ideas

(A) The first idea of the text is the question of the high priest, Caiphas, to the crowd, "What is your judgment?"

This is a crucial question when Jesus Christ was tried by the council of Jews in Jerusalem. An answer to this question determined the final destiny of Jesus. There is a need to examine the circumstances under which this question was asked. The circumstances of the question would require to answer the related and pertinent questions, such as: Who did ask the question? Was the question asked in fairness of the trial? Was the questioner free from malice and bias? Who did answer the question? Was the crowd free from hatred and bias? We shall attempt to answer these questions.

The first question is "Who did ask the question?" The questioner was the high priest, named Caiphas. The high priest was the chief executive officer of the council of the Jews in Jerusalem. He was trained in the scripture; therefore, he was given an authority to decide on religious questions. His opinion on religious issues would carry a weight.

By the virtue of his authority, Caiphas, the high priest, was presiding over the trial of Jesus. It is expected of a person who presides over a trial that he should be impartial and unbiased. Was Caiphas impartial and unbiased when he presided over the trial of Jesus?

The council of the Jews in Jerusalem was made of the high priest, chief priests, scribes, and the Pharisees. They became hostile to Jesus Christ, because Jesus boldly and publicly criticised hypocrisy of the Jewish leadership; and he corrected their wrong positions on many religious issues. Jesus thus challenged their authority and their interpretation of the scripture. Therefore, the council had thought to get rid of Jesus. They were looking for an excuse to put him on trial. Let us think of some of those events.

(1) Jesus Christ began his preaching ministry by his famous sermon on the mountain. In that sermon, he criticised conduct of scribes and Pharisees; and took different stands on modes of religious conduct, as follow:

> Thus, when you give alms, sound no trumpet before you, as the hypocrites do in the synagogues and in the streets, that they be praised by men. But when you give alms, do not let your left hand know what your right hand is doing, so that your alms may be in secret; and your Father who sees in secret will reward you.

> And when you pray, you must not be like the hypocrites; for they love to stand and pray in the synagogues and at the street corners, that they may be seen by men. Truly, I say to you, they have their reward. But when you pray, go into your room and shut the door and pray to your Father who is in secret; and your Father who sees in secret will reward you. (Mt. 6:2-6)

(2) The crowd was following Jesus Christ. When he sat at a table in the house, many tax collectors and sinners came and sat with Jesus and his disciples. The Pharisees did not approve of Jesus eating with the sinners. They asked a question to the disciples of Jesus, "Why does your teacher eat with tax collectors and sinners?" Jesus answered the question saying,

> Those who are well have no need of a physician, but those who are sick. Go and learn what this means, 'I desire mercy, and not sacrifice.' For I came not to call the righteous, but sinners. (Mt. 9:10-13)

In these words, Jesus justified his association with the sinners, on the basis of the scripture; and took a different position from that of the religious leaders of the Jews.

(3) Jesus entered the synagogue on the Sabbath day. A group of people presented a man with a withered hand to Jesus; and asked him, "Is it lawful to heal on the sabbath?" in order to accuse him of breaking the sabbath (Mt. 12:10). Jesus took a different stand on keeping the sabbath by saying:

> What man of you, if he has one sheep and it falls into a pit on the sabbath, will not lay hold of it and lift it out? Of how much more value is a man than a sheep! So it is lawful to do good on the sabbath. (Mt. 12:11-12)

Jesus healed the man on the sabbath. The Pharisees were extremely annoyed by this act of Jesus; and they took counsel against him how to destroy him (Mt. 12:14; Mk 3:6; Lk. 6:11). However, Jesus continued to heal the sick on sabbaths. He healed a woman, who had a spirit of infirmity for eighteen years, on a sabbath; he argued with the ruler of the synagogue; and condemned the hypocrisy of the religious leaders (Lk. 13:10-17). Jesus healed a man, who had dropsy, on a sabbath (Lk. 14:1-4).

(4) The scribes and Pharisees were closely watching behaviour of the disciples of Jesus. They came from Jerusalem to ask a question to Jesus, "Why do your disciples transgress the tradition of the elders? For they do not wash their hands when they eat." Jesus answered them, saying:

> And why do you transgress the commandment of God for the sake of your tradition? For God commanded, 'Honour your father and your mother,' and 'He who speaks evil of father or mother, let him surely die.' But you say, 'If any one tells his father or his mother, 'What you would have gained from me is given to God, he need not honour his father.' So, for the sake of your tradition, you have made void the word of God. You hypocrites! Well did Isaiah prophesy of you, when he said: 'this people honours me with their lips, but their heart is far from me; in vain do they worship me, teaching as doctrines the precepts of men.' (Mt. 15:3-9)

In these words, Jesus Christ condemned the scribes and Pharisees for breaking the commandments of God and acting as hypocrites. They were offended by the answer of Jesus (Mt. 15:12).

(5) After the triumphant entry on Sunday, Jesus entered the temple in Jerusalem; and overturned the tables of the moneychangers and the seats of those who sold pigeons. While cleansing the temple, he said to those merchants, "It is written, 'My house shall be called a house of prayer;' but you make it a den of robbers." (Mt. 21:13) On the following day, chief priests and the elders of the people went to Jesus; and asked him, "By what authority are you doing these things, and who gave you

this authority?" (Mt. 21:23) Then Jesus told them he would answer their question, if they answer his question: "The baptism of John, whence was it? From heaven or from men?" As they did not answer this question, Jesus did not answer their question.

(6) The Pharisees took a counsel to entangle Jesus in his talk. They sent their disciples with the Herodians, to ask Jesus a question: "Is it lawful to pay taxes to Caeser, or not?" (Mt. 22:17) Jesus answered them saying, "Render therefore to Caeser the things that are Caesar's, and to God the things that are God's." (Mt. 22:21) If Jesus would have advised them not to pay taxes to Caeser, he would have been guilty of opposing the rule of Roman power, or guilty of treason. Jesus knew their intention. He told them to pay taxes to the ruler of the land and to pay to God His share.

(7) In the presence of the crowd, Jesus denounced hypocrisy of the scribes and Pharisees; and he warned his disciples against them (Mt. 23:2-12,13-36).

As Jesus was very critical of the scribes and Pharisees, they were plotting to kill Jesus. The council of Jews in Jerusalem was deadly against him. The council decided to arrest Jesus by stealth and kill him (Mt. 26:3). Therefore, it sent its people with swords and clubs to arrest Jesus, with the help of Judas Iscariot, in the garden of Gethsemane.

The crowd arrested Jesus; and took him to the house of the high priest, Caiphas, to lay charges against Jesus. Caiphas encouraged the crowd to lay charges against Jesus. Many false witnesses came forward. But no one gave a testimony to charge Jesus with death penalty. When someone brought a false charge against Jesus (Mt.26:61), the high priest asked Jesus to respond it; but Jesus kept silence.

The high priest put Jesus under oath to tell them whether he was the Christ, the Son of God (Mt. 26:63). Jesus answered him, saying, "You have said so. But I tell you, hereafter you will see the Son of man seated at the right hand of Power, and coming on the clouds of heaven." (Mt. 26:64) The answer of Jesus was ambiguous. He did not directly deny the claim to be the Christ or the Son of God; and he did not affirm the claim clearly. He used the title 'Son of man' rather than 'Son of God' in his reply. He used the word 'Power' rather than 'God.' The council and the crowd were waiting for a clear-cut answer to lay a charge against Jesus. As Jesus did not give them a direct answer, the council had an option to release Jesus. The release of Jesus would have gone against the plot of the council to kill Jesus. The high priest had to say something on what Jesus said. The high priest acted dramatically. He tore his robes before he said something to lay a charge against Jesus. He said, "He has uttered blasphemy. Why do we still need witnesses? You have heard his blasphemy." (Mt. 26:65) The dramatic acting of the high priest had effect on the mind of the crowd. The high priest, who was presiding the hearing, who should have been impartial, charged Jesus with a religious crime of blasphemy. In his opinion, there was no need to have any more witness; the case was closed. Then the high priest asked the question, "What is your judgment?" (Mt. 26:66) The high priest, who was representing hostility and malice toward Jesus, asked this question to the crowd.

(B) The second idea of the text is the answer of the crowd saying, "He deserves death." When the high priest asked the crowd the question, "What is your judgment?," the crowd responded to the question of the high priest, saying, "He deserves death." (Mt. 26:66) The crowd was employed by the council to do the job of arresting Jesus and to accuse Jesus falsely. The crowd had to act according to the will of the council and not against wish of the council. It was to enforce the will and wish of the council. When the high priest asked the crowd, "What is your judgment?"he did not ask the question to have a negative answer from the crowd. He was waiting for a collective affirmative answer to his question. By the support of the crowd, his judgment became a judgment of a religious community. Thus, Jesus was falsely but collectively charged with a religious crime of blasphemy, deserving a death penalty.

The Jewish council decided to put Jesus to death. But the council was not allowed to execute a death penalty on anyone by the Roman power. Therefore, the council bound Jesus; and delivered him to Pontius Pilate (A. D. 26-36) the governor. The council members accused Jesus with a crime of treason. They said:

> We found this man perverting our nation, and forbidding us to give tribute to Caeser, and saying that he himself is Christ a king. (Lk. 23:2)

Then Pontius Pilate (A. D. 26-36) asked Jesus, "Are you the king of the Jews?" (Lk. 23:3). Jesus answered him, "You have said so." (Lk. 23:4) Jesus did not claim to be the king of the Jews. Pilate told the chief priests and the elders of the council that he did not find any crime in Jesus, punishable by death (Lk. 23:4). However, the crowd went on accusing Jesus that he was stirring up the people, teaching throughout Judea, from Galilee to Jerusalem (Lk. 23:5). When Pilate heard that Jesus was from Galilee, which was the jurisdiction of Herod Antipas (4 B. C. -A. D. 40), he sent Jesus to Herod Antipus, who was in Jerusalem at that time (Lk. 23:7).

Herod Antipas questioned Jesus at some length; but Jesus did not respond to those questions. The chief priests and Pharisees were accusing Jesus vehemently. Herod and his soldiers mocked Jesus and treated him with contempt. Herod sent Jesus back to Pontius Pilate (Lk. 23:10-11).

When Jesus was brought before Pontius Pilate the second time, by the chief priests, elders of the Jews, and Pharisees, Pilate said to them:

> You brought me this man as one who was perverting the people; and after examining him before you, behold, I did not find this man guilty of any of your charges against him; neither did Herod, for he sent him back to us. Behold, nothing deserving death has been done by him; I will therefore chastise him and release him. (Lk. 23:14-16)

Herod Antipas and Pontius Pilate did not find Jesus guilty of a crime, deserving a death penalty. Pilate wanted to release Jesus. Pilate, the governor, wished to use a custom of releasing a prisoner at the Passover feast. He asked the crowd, "Whom do you want me to release for you, Barabas or Jesus who is called Christ?" (Mt. 27:17) He was in favour of releasing Jesus, because he knew that the crowd had delivered Jesus out of their envy. The chief priests and the elders persuaded the crowd to ask for Barabas, a notorious prisoner, and to destroy Jesus (Mt. 27:20). Pilate again asked the crowd, "Which of the two do you want me to release for you?" (Mt. 27:21) As the chief priests and the elders tutored the crowd, the crowd said loudly, "Barabas." Then Pilate asked the crowd, "Then what shall I do with Jesus who is called Christ?" (Mt. 27:22) Then the crowd said, "Let him be crucified." (Mt. 27:22) The crowd said what they were tutored for by the religious council. Pilate tried to appeal to their common sense of justice and said, "Why, what evil has he done?" (Mt. 27:23) The crowd had no mind to reason and to respond to the question of Pilate. But they shouted all the more, "Let him be crucified." (Mt. 27:23)

Governor Pontius Pilate saw that he was gaining nothing from his defence of innocent Jesus; and the crowd was going to be violent, he took water and washed his hands before the crowd and said: "I am innocent of this man's blood; see to it yourselves." (Mt. 27:24) Then the crowd answered, "His blood be on us and on our children!" (Mt. 27:25) Pontius Pilate then released Barabas for the crowd; and he scourged Jesus and delivered him to be crucified (Mt. 27:26).

The religious council of the Jews wanted to kill Jesus. Therefore, the high priests, scribes, elders of the people, and Pharisees were trying to find something against Jesus that they might justify their hatred in killing Jesus. They put Jesus on a trial. But the trial was not fair; it was intended to put Jesus to death. The council did not follow the principles of justice and truth, when it put Jesus on the trial. The council denied justice and fairness to Jesus.

Pontius Pilate and Herod Antipas, who represented secular court, did not treat Jesus fairly. Though they found Jesus innocent, they were not in position to protect Jesus and release him. When Pontius Pilate found the crowd was going to be violent, he delivered Jesus to the crowd that it may crucify Jesus. Jesus was offered as a sacrifice in order to keep peace in Jerusalem. The secular court denied justice and fairness to Jesus.

From a judicial point of view, Jesus Christ was not legally and properly treated by the authorities, which were supposed to uphold the law of the LORD God and of the land. What is the justification of the death of innocent Jesus from a biblical point of view? We should answer this question.

Neither the religious law and authority of the Jews nor the secular law and authority of the Roman Empire proved Jesus guilty of corporal punishment. However, Jesus was sentenced to be crucified. This indicates that there is a possibility of structural injustice in religious institutes and in secular judicial systems. The trial of Jesus was a mockery of the justice system.

There is an explanation of the death of innocent Jesus. Prophet Isaiah had prophesied about the suffering servant of God, when he wrote these words, as follow:

> He was despised and rejected by men; a man of sorrow, and acquainted with grief;... surely he has borne our griefs and carried our sorrows, yet we esteemed him stricken, smitten by God, and afflicted. But he was wounded for our transgressions, he was bruised for our iniquities; upon him was the chastisement that made us whole, and with his stripes we are healed. All we like sheep have gone astray; we have turned every one to his own way; and the LORD has laid on him the iniquity of us all. He was oppressed, and he was afflicted, yet he opened not his mouth; like a lamb that is led to the slaughter, and like a sheep that before its shearers is dumb, so he opened not his mouth. (Is. 53:3-7)

St. Peter reflected on the death of Jesus Christ, in the following words, similar of those of Isaiah:

> He committed no sin; no guile was found on his lips. When he was reviled, he did not revile in return; when he suffered, he did not threaten; but he trusted to him who judges justly. He himself bore our sins in his body on the tree, that we might die to sin and live to righteousness. By his wounds you have been healed. For you were straying like sheep, but have now returned to the Shepherd and Guardian of your souls. (I Pet. 2:22-25)

St. Paul similarly explained the mystery of the death of Jesus Christ, who was innocent, in the following words:

For I delivered to you as of first importance what I also received, that Christ died for our sins in accordance with the scripture, that he was buried, that he was raised on the third day in accordance with the scriptures. (I Cor. 15:3-4)

Conclusion

Jesus Christ was denied justice by the religious and civil authorities; and they had parts in crucifying the innocent. The trial and death of Jesus Christ could be understood in the light of the scripture. He died for redemption of sinners, in accordance to the will of God.

Recommended Hymns from the Methodist Hymnal

176 'Man of sorrows! What a name'

178 'When my love to Christ grows weak,'

180 'There is a green hill far away,'

Recommended Responsive Reading from the Methodist Hymnal
74 (pp. 416f.),

Recommended Responsive Reading from *A Worship Manual for Scriptural or Methodist Order of Service*
76 (pp. 189-190).

Chapter 9

'Necessity of True Repentance,' 'Conditional Salvation.'

Scripture

Luke 13:1-9

Exodus 9:27-28; 10:16-17

I Samuel 24:10-11, 17-18; 26:21

Psalms 51:1-13

Romans 3:10-18

Text: Luke 13:5

A Few Versions of the Text, Luke 13:5

I tell you, no; but unless you repent you will all likewise perish. *New king James Version*

I tell you, Nay: but, except ye repent, ye shall all likewise perish. *Explanatory Notes Upon the New Testament*

I tell you, No; but unless you repent you will all likewise perish. *Revised Standard Version*

I tell you, no! But unless you repent, you too will all perish. *New International Version*

I tell you they were not; but unless you repent, you will all of you come to the same end. *The New English Bible*

Not at all! And you, too, will perish unless you repent. *The Living Bible Illustrated*

No! I can guarantee that they weren't. But if you don't turn to God and change the way you think and act, then you, too, will all die. *God's Word*

Introduction

During the civil war, President Abraham Lincoln (1809-1865) wrote: "It is the duty of nations as well as men to own their dependence upon the overruling power of God; to confess their sins and transgressions in humble sorrow, yet with assured hope that genuine repentance will lead to mercy and pardon; and to recognize the sublime truth announced in the Holy Scriptures and proven by all history, that those nations only are blessed whose God is the Lord. The awful calamity of civil war which now desolates the land may be but a punishment inflicted upon us for our presumptuous sins, to the needful end of our national reformation as a whole people. Intoxicated with unbroken success, we have become too self-sufficient to feel the necessity too proud to pray to the God that made us. It behoves us, then, to humble ourselves before the offended Power, to confess our national sins, and to pray for clemency and forgiveness." Abraham Lincoln designated Thursday the 30th day of April 1863, as a day of national humiliation, fasting and prayer.[1]

President Abraham Lincoln, by his writing and proclamation reaffirmed the necessity of repentance in the life of nations and of individuals. He alluded to the Holy Scriptures, which he meant the Bible.

Introduction of the Text

The Bible has made man's salvation conditional. Salvation of man is absolutely conditional. It is conditional in the sense that man has to repent of his sins and spiritual wickedness. Without repentance, there is no spiritual salvation. Jesus Christ, in his teaching put emphasis on the necessity of true repentance, in these words:

I tell you, No; but unless you repent you will all likewise perish.
(Luke 13: 5)

This is the text of our meditation now.

The Context of the Text

Jesus was surrounded by people. They told Jesus about the event that Pontius Pilate (A. D. 26-36) killed some Galileans who went to offer sacrifices and he mingled the blood of those Galileans with their sacrifices. Those people presumed that those Galileans were worse sinners than the rest of the Galileans, therefore, they were killed by Pontius Pilate. Against this presupposition, Jesus had to take a stand. Therefore, he asked them a question, "Do you think that these Galileans were worse sinners than all the other Galileans, because they suffered thus?" Jesus Christ did not wait for their answer. But he answered them saying, "I tell you, No; but unless you repent you will all likewise perish?" (Lk. 13:3)

The crowd mentioned this disaster to Jesus Christ, in which Pontius Pilate killed some Galileans. We have not got enough historical records about the event. Biblical scholars speculate about the event thus. Galileans were highly inflammable people; therefore, they used to get involved in any political trouble. They used to oppose Roman officials, therefore, the Romans had to rule the Galileans with iron fist and firmness. At the time of Pontius Pilate, some Jews revolted. When Jews gathered in the temple to slaughter their sacrifices, Pilate ordered his soldiers to slay some violent Galileans because he suspected of them being insurrectionaries. Some Jews escaped the disaster. They thought of the Galileans, who were slain in the disaster, as the people who suffered death because of their sins. They also thought of the Jews, who escaped from the disaster, as the people, who were righteous and needed no repentance. Jesus repudiated this popular concept that suffering was the consequence of sin. He interpreted the event in terms of that the befallen Galileans were to serve a warning to other people that they should repent before it would be too late, otherwise they too would perish in a like manner.

Jesus Christ continued his argument with the people by citing another similar disaster. Pontius Pilate confiscated the temple treasury. Out of that money, he was paying wages to eighteen persons to build a tower of his aqueduct (an artificial channel carrying water across country). The tower of Siloam fell on those eighteen persons; and they were killed instantly. Some Jews thought of the disaster as punishment by death to those who were sinners. Jesus repudiated this popular notion and told the people: "I tell you, No; but unless you repent you will all likewise perish." (Lk. 13:5)

Jesus Christ repeated the verse (Lk. 13:5) before (Lk. 13:3) in order to emphasize the necessity of true repentance in order to be saved from similar disasters.

An Analysis of the Text

This text has two ideas. (A) The first idea is the definite answer of Jesus to the people saying, "No," against their popular notion.

(B) The second idea is that Jesus told the people, saying, "unless you repent you will all likewise perish."

An Exposition of the Ideas

(A) The first idea of the text is the definite answer of Jesus to the people saying, "No," against their popular notion. The popular misconception among the Jews about the mishap was that those who were slaughtered by Pontius Pilate in the temple were secretly bad persons. Otherwise, God would not have permitted Pontius Pilate to cut those persons off savagely. The Jews did not acknowledge them to be martyrs; but they supposed them to be malefactors. Jesus Christ saw a spiteful innuendo of Jews, when they told him the event how Pilate killed some Galileans. Jesus did not approve the interpretation of the tragedy, because the great sufferers were condemned as great sinners. Jesus asked them a question: "Do you think that these Galileans were worse sinners than all the other Galileans, because they suffered thus?" (Lk. 13:2) In order to make them understand his point, Jesus cited a similar event of sudden death of eighteen persons from Jerusalem, due to collapsing of the tower of Siloam. Jesus then asked them a similar question, "Do you think that they were worse offenders than all the others who dwelt in Jerusalem?" (Lk. 13:4) Jesus answered those questions with certainty and with his authority, saying, "I tell you, No; but unless you repent you will all likewise perish." (Lk. 13:5)

Jesus Christ wanted to teach a new perspective on calamities that people should not judge others' sins by their sufferings in this world, because many righteous persons are persecuted as gold is thrown in the furnace to be purified, and not as rubbish to be consumed. We should not be harsh in judging others, otherwise we would be judged in the same way (Mt. 7:1).[2]

Jesus Christ wanted the people refrained from passing moral judgments on others. They should introspect and repent for their sins and ask God's forgiveness; otherwise they would perish eternally, as others perished out of this world. In other words, Jesus put emphasis on true repentance for sins, leading to the eternal salvation.

There is a need of true repentance, because without it nobody would be saved. We have to repent not only for the sins we have committed; but also for our tendency to commit sin. In the sight of God, nobody is pure and righteous. St. Paul continued the teaching of Jesus Christ, when he argued on the basis of the scripture, as follows:

> None is righteous, no, not one; no one understands, no one seeks for God. All have turned aside, together they have gone wrong; no one does good, not even one, their throat is an open grave, they use their tongues to deceive. The venom of asps is under their lips. Their mouth is full of curses and bitterness. Their feet are swift to shed blood, in their paths are ruin and misery, and the way of peace they do not know. There is no fear of God before their eyes. (Rom. 3:10-18)

All of us are sinners. Therefore, we need to repent of our sins, committed by deed, word, and thought. Unless we repent, we will perish as others perished because of their sins, and their reluctance to repent, and their unwillingness to turn to God. If we repent truly, God will forgive us our sins and grant us eternal salvation. This spiritual thought will be explained in the following pages.

(B) The second idea of the text is that Jesus told the people, saying, "unless you repent you will all likewise perish." Jesus Christ put emphasis on true repentance by which sinners are saved. True repentance is not a superficial feeling of sorrow, which last for some time and which does not cause any effect on an offender. But it is a deep sorrow, lasting long time and causing a permanent change in behaviour of a person. Let us examine a few examples in order to distinguish superficial sorrow from true repentance.

(1) When the LORD God sent hail on Egypt, destroying every tree and plant in the field, Pharaoh called Moses and Aaron and said to them,

> I have sinned this time; the LORD is in the right, and I and my people are in the wrong. Entreat the LORD; for there has been enough of this thunder and hail; I will let you go, and you shall stay no longer.
> (Ex. 9:27-28)

After the disaster, Pharaoh's heart was hardened; and he did not keep his promise, allowing Israelites to leave Egypt.

On another occasion, when God sent locusts on Egypt, eating all plants away, Pharaoh called Moses and Aaron and said to them:

> I have sinned against the LORD your God, and against you. Now therefore, forgive my sin I pray you, only this once, and entreat the LORD your God only to remove this death from me. (Ex. 10:16-17)

After this disaster, Pharaoh's heart was hardened. This happened other times and finally Pharaoh's army, which was trying to recapture Israelites, was drowned in the Red Sea, because Pharaoh, Ramses II (1301-1234 B. C.) never truly repented of his wrong doings; he had temporary sorrow all other times.

(2) King Saul (1044-1004 B. C.) was attempting to kill David (1002-692 B. C.), because he thought of David as a real threat to his throne. When David was hiding in the wilderness of Engedi, King Saul took 3,000 well-trained persons with him to capture David. David and his people were hiding in a cave. King Saul went in the cave to relieve himself. David was in position to kill Saul, but he stealthily cut off the skirt of Saul's robe. After this, David went away at a distance and spoke loudly to King Saul, thus:

> I will not put forth my hand against my lord; for he is the LORD's anointed. See, my father, see the skirt of your robe in my hand; for by the fact that I cut off the skirt of your robe, and did not kill you, you may know and see that there is no wrong or treason in my hands. I have not sinned against you, though you hunt my life to take it. (I Sam. 24:10-11)

Then King Saul replied to David, as follows:

> You are more righteous that I; for you have repaid me good, whereas I have repaid you evil. And you have declared this day how you have dealt with me, in that you did not kill me when the LORD put me into your hands. (I Sam. 24:17-18)

King Saul felt sorrow superficially for his wicked action to kill David. After some days, King Saul again went to capture David, when David was hiding in the wilderness of Zip. At midnight, King Saul was fast asleep among his soldiers. David took the spear and jar of water from King Saul; and he did not kill Saul. David went on the top of the mountain and called Abner, the commander in chief, loudly; and told him that he took away the spear and jar from King Saul; and he did not kill Saul. King Saul heard their conversation; and he said to David:

> I have done wrong; return, my son David; for I will no more do you harm, because my life was precious in your eyes this day; behold, I have played the fool, and have erred exceedingly. (I Sam. 26:21)

David returned the spear and the jar to King Saul. But Saul kept on attempting to kill David. Saul never had true repentance; he had temporary sorrows.

(3) True repentance is deep and genuine sorrow; it causes change in the behaviour of the repentant. King David committed an adultery with Bathsheba, and he killed her husband by a plot. King David was guilty of sins of adultery and murder. God sent Nathan, the prophet, to condemn David and to pronounce His judgment. King David realized his sins and repented for his sins. He sincerely asked the LORD God to forgive his sins, and to give him a clean heart, in the following words:

> Have mercy on me, O God, according to thy steadfast love; according to thy abundant mercy blot out my transgressions. Wash me thoroughly from my iniquity, and cleanse me from my sin! For I know my transgressions, and my sin is ever before me. Against thee, and thee only, have I sinned, and done that which is evil in thy sight, so that thou art justified in thy sentence and blameless in thy judgment. Behold, I was brought forth in iniquity and in sin did my mother conceive me. Behold, thou desireth truth in the inward being; therefore teach me wisdom in my secret heart. Purge me with hyssop, and I shall be clean; wash me, and I shall be whiter than snow.... Create in me a clean heart O God, and put a new and right spirit within me. Cast me not away from thy presence, and take not thy holy Spirit from me. Restore to me the joy of thy salvation, and uphold me with a willing spirit. Then I will teach transgressors thy ways, and sinners will return to thee. (Ps. 51:1-13)

King David expressed his deep sorrow in the appropriate way. His way of expressing sorrow was a way of an individual.

(4) As an individual sinner is required to express his or her sorrow sincerely and is expected to demonstrate a change in his or her attitude and action, the nations are also asked to repent collectively and ask for God's pardon and mercy. On behalf of the people of Judah, Ezra expressed their deep sorrow in the following words:

> O my God, I am ashamed and blush to lift my face to thee, my God, for our iniquities have risen higher than our heads, and our guilt has mounted up to the heavens. Form the days of our fathers to this day we have been in great guilt; and for our iniquities we, our kings, and our priests have been given into the hand of the kings of the lands, to the sword, to captivity, to plundering, and to utter shame, as at this day. But now for a brief moment favour has been shown by the LORD our God, to leave us a remnant, and to give us secure hold within his holy place,

> that our God may brighten our eyes and grant us a little reviving in our
> bondage. For we are bondmen; yet our God has not forsaken us in our
> bondage, but has extended to us his steadfast love before the kings of
> Persia, to grant us some reviving to set up the house of our God, to repair
> its ruins, and to give up protection in Judea and Jerusalem. (Ezra 9:6-9)

(5) When the church at Corinth did something wrong, St. Paul had to
write a letter to the congregation to guide them in a proper way. The
tone of the letter was harsh. After sending the letter, he wrote to them:

> For even if I made you sorry with my letter, I do not regret it (though I
> did regret it), for I see that letter grieved you, though only for a while.
> As it is, I rejoice, not because you were grieved, but because you were
> grieved into repenting, for you felt a godly grief, so that you suffered
> no loss through us. For godly grief produces a repentance that leads to
> salvation and brings no regret, but worldly grief produces death. For see
> what earnestness this godly grief has produced in you, what eagerness to
> clear yourselves, what indignation, what alarm, what longing, what zeal,
> what punishment! At every point you have proved yourselves guiltless
> in the matter. (II Cor. 7:8-11)

In this passage, St. Paul spoke of "godly grief" which makes people
repent and leads them to salvation. It produces a change in the heart
and action of the repentant. It is like the prodigal son, who returned
to his pardoning father, with a real change in his heart (Lk. 15:17-18).
The true repentance leads to salvation. Jesus Christ put emphasis on
true repentance, leading to eternal salvation, in his teaching.

Conclusion

Jesus Christ gave a new perspective to the people to look at the sufferings
of others. He taught them not to pass judgment on others when they
suffer; and He asked the people to repent for their sins, otherwise they
would perish as others perished before them.

Recommended Hymns from the Methodist Hymnal

347 'Come, O Thou all-victorious Lord,'

351 'I hear Thy welcome voice'

498 'Rock of Ages, cleft for me,'

543 'Hear, Thou my prayer, O Lord,'

Recommended Responsive Reading from the Methodist Hymnal
#35 (p. 398),

Recommended Responsive Reading from *A Worship Manual for Scriptural or Methodist Order of Service*
28 (pp. 115-116).

Endnotes

[1] Paul Lee Tan, *Encyclopedia of 7700 Illustrations: Signs of the Times,* #4965.

[2] *The NIV Matthew Henry Commentary in One Volume,* (Grand Rapids, Michigan: Zondervan Publishing House, 1992) p.264.

Chapter 10

'A Form of the Spiritual Worship,' 'Worshipping God in Spirit and in Truth,' 'Universal Way of Worshipping God in Jesus Christ,' 'Universalized, Personalized, and Particularized Way of Worshipping God.'

Scripture

John 4:16-30

Deuteronomy 27:12

I Kings 8:27; 9:3-9, 26-37; 12:26-33; 13:2

II Kings 15:9, 24, 28-29; 17:1-16; 23:15-17; 24:10-16; 25:8-17

II Chronicles 36:22-23

Ezra 1:1-4; 2:64-65; 3:8; 4:3, 5, 24; 6:15

Nehemiah 13:28

Isaiah 66:1-2, 18-23

Zephaniah 2:11

Malachi 1:11

Matthew 18:20; 24:1-2, 4-5Mark 13:1-2, 6

Luke 21:5-6, 8

Acts 2:38-42

I Corinthians 3:16-17; 6:17-20

II Corinthians 1:2; 5:4; 6:14-18

I John 3:23-24

Text: John 4:21

A few Versions of the Text, John 4:21

Jesus said to her, 'Woman, believe Me, the hour is coming when you will neither on this mountain, nor in Jerusalem, worship the Father. *New King James Version*

Jesus saith to her, Woman, believe me, the hour cometh, when ye shall neither in this mountain, nor at Jerusalem, worship the Father. *Explanatory Notes Upon the New Testament*

Jesus said to her, 'Woman, believe me, the hour is coming when neither on this mountain nor in Jerusalem, will you worship the Father. *Revised Standard Version*

Jesus declared, 'Believe me, woman, a time is coming when you will worship the Father neither on this mountain nor in Jerusalem. *New International Version*

'Believe Me,' said Jesus, the time is coming when you will worship the Father neither on this mountain, nor in Jerusalem. *The New English Bible.*

Jesus replied, ' The time is coming, ma'ma, when we will no longer be concerned about whether to worship the Father here or in Jerusalem. *The Living Bible Illustrated*

Jesus told her, 'Believe Me. A time is coming when you Samaritans won't be worshipping the Father on this mountain or in Jerusalem.' *God's Word*

Introduction

Temples, Synagogues, Mosques, and Churches are thought to be holy places because the believers of these religions- Hindus, Jews, Muslim, and Christians respectively- believe that their gods are specially present in those abodes. The sites of the holy building get emotional attachment of the believers. The right to preserve and protect those holy buildings creates social and political turmoils.

In the several years, Hindus from Ayodhya, Uttar Pradesh, India, organized a political movement, claiming that a Muslim Mosque in Ayodhya was built on the site where Rama, a god of Hindus, was born. In other words, Muslims destroyed a temple of Rama; and turned it into a Mosque. Therefore, militant Hindus and their political leaders wanted to repossess the site and to restore the temple of worshipping Rama. They have destroyed the mosque; and they might build a temple there.

The first temple of the Jews was built by King Solomon (962-922 B. C.) in 960 B. C. The site was the central place of worshipping the LORD God, Yahweh for the Jews. The first temple was destroyed by King Nebuchadnezzar in 586 B. C. King Cyrus (539-530 B. C.), the king of Persia made a decree that Jews return to Jerusalem and rebuild the temple in Jerusalem (Ezra 1:1-4) in 538 B. C. Zerubbabel and other Jews went to Jerusalem and started to rebuild their second temple, on a smaller scale in ca. 537 B. C. (Ezra 3). Zerubbable became a governor of Israel. He helped the people of Judah to rebuild the altar and the temple (Ezra 3; Hag. 1-2; Zec. 4). King Herod (37- 4 B. C.) enlarged the second temple. This temple was completely destroyed by Titus the Roman general in 70.

Omar Ibn Al-Khatab conquered Palestine in 636. The temple area had been under the control of Muslims since seventh century. The temple area is occupied by the Muslim Mosque known as 'The Dome of the Rock,' otherwise known as the 'Mosque of Omar.' This mosque was built by Omar Ibn Al-Khatab, after his conquest of Palestine. This mosque is the second most sacred shrine for Muslims. Israel is now in control of the temple area. But orthodox Jews are not allowed to cross the area. The Chief Rabbinate Council issued the prohibition in accordance with *halacha,* that Jews may approach the Wailing Wall by the way of the Dung Gate from the north or the Jaffa Gate from the west, until the Jewish temple is rebuilt. This prohibition prevents clashes between Arabs and Jews in the city of Jerusalem.[1] Militant Jews want to repossess the site and to rebuild the temple on its original site. This restoration project would involve violent actions.

Introduction of the Text

The sacred sites sometimes become controversial matters even among the people, who apparently serve the same God. Jesus Christ was presented with a problem over which site should be the place of worshipping God, by a woman. Jesus Christ provided the answer to this dilemma, in his conversation with the woman, in the following words:

> **Jesus said to her, 'Woman, believe me, the hour is coming when neither on this mountain nor in Jerusalem, will you worship the Father,** (John 4:21)

This is the text of our meditation now.

The Context of the Text

There was a short cut from Judah to Galilee through Samaria. But Jews always used to go around Samaria in order to go to Galilee, because there was hostility between Jews and Samaritans. Jesus and his disciples left Judah for Galilee. But they did not follow the route which other Jews generally took. They wanted to use the short cut. They decided to pass through Samaria. They reached to Sychar, formerly known as Shechem, a city of Samaria. In that city was the field which Jacob gave to his son Joseph (Gen. 33:19; 48:22; Jos. 24:32). In that field was a well, dug by Jacob; it was the well for public. Jesus sat at the well and his disciples went into the city to buy food for them.

It was noon when Jesus sat at the well. At that time a Samaritan women came to draw water from the well. The woman saw a Jew sitting at the well. Jesus approached the woman; and asked for water to drink. The woman was puzzled over the request of a Jew, because the Jews had no dealing with Samaritans (Jn 4:9; Ezra 4:3-6). The woman asked the Jew the question, saying: 'How is it that you, a Jew, ask a drink of me, a woman of Samaria?' (Jn 4:8) She did not know who that Jew was. Jesus Christ had a desire to reveal himself to be the anticipated Messiah to her. In their conversation, Jesus touched upon her personal life; thereafter she realized him to be a prophet. Then the woman started to ask a question about the controversial importance of site of worshipping God. She pointed out a religious controversy about the site of worshipping God, saying: "Our fathers worshipped on this mountain; and you say that in Jerusalem is the place where men ought to worship." (Jn 4:20) In other words, the woman asked Jesus Christ which of the two sites was the appropriate site to worship. The writer of the gospel recorded the answer of Jesus Christ to this controversial question, in the words as follow:

> Jesus said to her, 'Woman, believe me, the hour is coming when neither on this mountain nor in Jerusalem, will you worship the Father, (Jn 4:21)

This is the text, within its historical background.

An Analysis of the Text

This text has three thoughts. (A) The first idea is the prediction or prophecy of Jesus Christ that the time is coming when the true worshippers would worship God the Father in a different way.

(B) The true worshippers would not worship God the Father on this mountain [Gerazim].

(C) The true worshippers would not worship God the Father in Jerusalem.

An Exposition of the Textual Ideas

We shall deal with these ideas in the reverse order. We shall first deal with Jerusalem as a worship site for the Jews. Then we shall deal with the creation of the worship site on the Mount Gerazim and its destruction. Then we shall deal with the prophesy of Jesus Christ that true worshippers would not worship God either on the Mount Gerazim or in Jerusalem, but they would worship God the Father in truth and in spirit.

(C) The true worshippers would not worship God the Father in Jerusalem. King Solomon (962-922 B. C.) built the first temple for worshipping the LORD God at Jerusalem, according to the will of God. God approved the site as the place of worship and of offering sacrifices to Him. The permanence of the temple was made conditional by God Himself when the LORD God appeared to Solomon second time at Gibeon and said these words to King Solomon:

> I have heard your prayer and supplication, which you have made before me; I have consecrated this house which you have built, and put my name there for ever; my eyes and my heart will be there for all time. And as for you, if you walk before me, as David your father walked, with integrity of heart and uprightness, doing according to all that I have commanded you, and keeping my statutes and my ordinances, then I will establish your royal throne over Israel for ever, as I promised David your father, saying, 'There shall not fail you a man upon the throne of Israel.' But if you turn aside from following me, you or your children, and do not keep my commandments and my statutes which I have set before you, but go and serve other gods and worship them, then I will cut off Israel from the land which I have given them; and the house which I have consecrated for my name I will cast out of my sight; and Israel will become a proverb and a byword among all peoples. And this house will become a heap of ruins; everyone passing by it will be astonished, and will hiss; and they will say, 'Why has the LORD done thus to this land and to this house?' Then they will say, 'Because they forsook the LORD their God who brought their fathers out of the land of Egypt, and laid hold of other gods, and worshipped them and served them; therefore the LORD has brought all this evil upon them.' (I Kg. 9:3-9)

The people of Israel and their kings failed to keep the commandments of God, therefore the LORD God was angry with them. King Solomon married princes of other nations and he built shrines for their gods and offered sacrifices (I Kg. 11:1-9). Therefore, God decided to divide the kingdom of Israel into two kingdoms- the kingdom of Judah and the kingdom of Israel- during the reign of King Solomon's son, Rehoboam (922-915 B. C.) (I Kg. 11:9-13). Prophet Ahijah went to see Jeroboam

(922-901 B. C.), a servant of Solomon, and told him that God would make him a king over the kingdom of Israel (I Kg. 11:26-37). Jeroboam established the kingdom of Israel with the support of the ten tribes of Israel.

The kings of Judah and the people sinned against the LORD God and God used King Nebuchadnezzar (605-562 B. C.), a ruler of Babylon, to punish the people of Judah. King Nebuchadnezzar besieged Jerusalem, and took King Jehoiachin (598 B. C.) the king of Judah and many officials and ten thousand captives to Babylon; he carried off all the treasure of the house of God and golden vessels of the temple, which King Solomon had made, in ca. 598 B. C. (II Kg. 24:10-16). When King Zedekiah (598-587 B. C.), the king of Judah, rebelled against King Nebuchadnezzar, he came second time in 587 B. C. and burned the temple of God and palace, and houses of the people; his army broke down the walls of Jerusalem; he took many people as his captives; he carried all the vessels of the temple to Babylon (II Kg. 25:8-17).

God raised King Cyrus (539-530 B. C.), the king of Persia, to bring back the exiles into the promised land and to restore the temple and the walls of Jerusalem. King Cyrus made a decree that Jews to return to Jerusalem and rebuild the temple in Jerusalem (II Chr. 36:22-23; Ezra 1:1-4) in ca. 538 B. C. King Cyrus brought all the vessels and utensils of the temple from Babylon to Jerusalem and handed them over to Sheshbazzar, the prince of Judah (Ezra 1:8-11). Zerubbabel and other Jews went to Jerusalem in ca. 537 B. C. to rebuild their second temple (Ezra 2:64-65), on a smaller scale. King Herod (37-4 B. C.) enlarged the second temple. This was the temple at the time of Jesus Christ.

When Jesus came out of the temple, one of his disciples said to him, "Look, Teacher, what wonderful stones and what wonderful buildings!" Then Jesus prophesied, "Do you see these great buildings? There will not be left here one stone upon another, that will not be thrown away." (Mk 13:1-2; Mt. 24:1-2; Lk. 21:5-6) This temple was completely destroyed by Titus the Roman general in A. D. 70. The site of the second temple had been under the control of Muslims since seventh century. The temple area is occupied by the Muslim Mosque known as 'The Dome of the Rock,' otherwise known as the 'Mosque of Omar.' This mosque was built by Omar Ibn Al-Khatab, after his conquest of Palestine. Orthodox Jews cannot enter this area; they cannot worship in this area.

(B) The true worshippers would not worship God the Father on this mountain [Gerazim]. The kingdom of Israel was divided into two kingdoms- the kingdom of Judah and the kingdom of Israel. Jeroboam (922-901 B. C.) became the first king of the kingdom of Israel. King Jeroboam thought that his kingdom would turn back to the house of David if his people go up to Jerusalem to offer sacrifices to the LORD God, and his people would kill him and return the kingdom of Israel to Rehoboam (I Kg. 12:26-28). Therefore, he took a counsel and made two calves of gold and told the people that these were their gods who brought them out of the bondage of Egypt. He set those images in Bethel and Dan. King Jeroboam built houses on high places, and appointed priests who were not Levites. He appointed a day of feast, similar to that of it in Jerusalem. He offered sacrifices to the idols on altars and burnt incense to them. He led the people of Israel to commit a horrible sin against the LORD God (I Kg.12:29-33). A prophet from Judah went to Bethel. King Jeroboam was standing by the altar to burn incense. The prophet said:

> 'O altar, altar, thus says the LORD: Behold a son shall be born to the house
> of David, Josiah by name; and he shall sacrifice upon you the priests of
> the high places who burn incense upon you, and men's bones shall be
> burned upon you. (I Kg. 13:2)

This prophesy was fulfilled when King Josiah (640-609 B. C.) carried a religious reform movement in the heart of the kingdom of Israel; and he defiled those altars by killing the priests and pouring ashes of bones, taken from the tombs, on the altars in Bethel and in Dan (II Kg. 23:15-17). King Josiah destroyed all high places in the kingdom of Israel.

Kings of the kingdom of Israel, after Jeroboam, - Nadab (901-900), Baasha (900-877 B. C.), Elah (877-876 B. C.), Omri (876-869 B. C.), Ahab (869-850 B. C.), Azariah (850-849 B. C.), Joram (849-842 B. C.), Jehu (842-815 B. C.), Joahaz (815-801 B. C.), Joash (801-786 B. C.), and Jeroboam (786-746 B. C.) did not obey the LORD God. They perpetuated sin of King Jeroboam. King Zechariah (746-745 B. C.), the son of King Jeroboam (786-746 B. C.) acted wickedly (II Kg. 15:9). King Gadi did the same thing (II Kg. 15:18). King Pekahiah (738-737 B. C.) (II Kg. 15:24), King Pekah (737-732 B. C.) (II Kg. 15:28) and King Hoshea (732-724 B. C.) (II Kg. 17:2) worshipped other idols. They kindled the wrath of God. God punished them through the foreign rulers. In the days of King Pekah (737-732 B. C.), king of Israel, King Tigalth-pileser III, the king of Assyria came up against the kingdom of Israel, he captured many cites and took Israelites as captives to Assyria (II Kg 15:29). In the days of King Hoshea (732-724 B. C.), the king of Israel, King Shalmaneser V (727-722 B. C.), the king of Assyria, captured the cities of the kingdom of Israel; and he took many Israelites as captives to Assyria and placed them in the cities of Medes (II Kg. 17:1-6) in ca. 724 B. C. God raised King Cyrus (539-530 B. C.), the king of Persia, to bring back the exiles into the promised land, and to restore the temple and the walls of Jerusalem. King Cyrus made a decree that Jews to return to Jerusalem and rebuild the temple in Jerusalem (II Chr. 36:22-23; Ezra 1:1-4) in ca. 538 B. C. After the edict, Jews from various provinces of Persian empire started to go back to Judah and Jerusalem. In that year 49, 897 Jews returned (Ezra 2:64-65). Zerubbabel was among them. He and other priests undertook to restore the temple in 537 B. C. (Ezra 3:8). While they were restoring the temple of the LORD God, Samaritans approached Zerubbabel and other heads of the people of Judah and offered help to build the temple. But Zerubbabel and others said to the Samaritans:

> You have nothing to do with us in building a house to our God; but we alone will build to the LORD, the God of Israel, as king Cyrus the king of Persia had commanded us. (Ezra 4:3)

The Samaritans felt insulted; they tried to stop the work; they attacked the workers and hired counsellors to frustrate their purpose (Ezra 4:5, 24). The work was stopped about seventeen years. The work resumed in the second year of King Darius the great (522-486 B. C.) (Ezra 4:24; Hag. 1:15), under the leadership of prophet Haggai. The work went on four years; it was completed in 516 B. C. (Ezra 6:15)

As Samaritans opposed building the temple and the walls of Jerusalem, they were not allowed to enter the temple at Jerusalem. They broke off from the rest of Jews. When religious reforms were taking place at Jerusalem, Manasseh, the son-in-law of Sanballat the Heronite, went off to found a community in Samaria in 432 B. C. (Neh. 13:28). This community built a temple on Mount Gerizim in ca. 332 B. C. Then the community started to rewrite the first five books of Moses, justifying the temple on Mount Gerizim as the central place of worship and sacrifices. Gerizim was known as the mountain of blessing (Deut. 11:29) as Moses pronounced God's blessings on the people who would keep God's law (Deut. 27:12). An existence of the two holy temples created a controversy as to which should be the central place of worship and sacrifice. John Hyrcanus I (134-104 B. C.), a Maccabees, destroyed the temple on Mount Gerizim in 128 B. C. However, the controversy continued to exist. Therefore, the woman, who met Jesus Christ at Jacob's well, referred to the controversy, saying: "Our fathers worshipped on this mountain [Gerizim]; and you [Jews] say that in Jerusalem is the place men ought to worship." (Jn 4:20) How did Jesus Christ answer her question is our next textual idea.

(A) The third idea is the prediction or prophecy of Jesus Christ that the time is going to come when the true worshippers would worship God the Father in a different way. The true worshippers would not worship the LORD God either on Mount Gerizim or in Jerusalem. Their way of worship would not be confined to these temples. Their worship would be in spirit and truth. Jesus Christ answered the woman saying:

> The hour is coming, and now is, when the true worshippers will worship the Father in spirit and truth. (Jn 4:23)

These words of Jesus Christ clearly stated that the time, that was to come, has come and has started from the moment Jesus declared its arrival. Jesus proclaimed the arrival of the time. In other words, the arrival of the Messiah, Jesus Christ inaugurated the new era of worshipping God the Father in spirit and in truth. Further, in his reply, Jesus Christ did not mention where the worshippers would worship; but he stated the way they would worship. The way of worshipping God the Father would be a new way in terms of no limit to the sites of worship. There would be no need of a central place of worship. It will be anywhere and everywhere or rather universal.

God is the Spirit and He is omnipresent. Therefore, His Spirit cannot be confined to any particular sacred site; He should be worshipped everywhere. The omnipresence of the LORD God was recognized by King Solomon when he built the first temple for the LORD God. He said:

> But will God indeed dwell on the earth? Behold, heaven and the highest heaven cannot contain thee; how much less this house which I have built! (I Kg. 8:27)

Prophet Isaiah heard God saying about His omnipresence in the following words:

> Heaven is my house and the earth is my footstool; what is the house which you would build for me, and what is the place of my rest? All these things my hand has made, and so all these things are mine, says the LORD. (Is. 66:1-2)

Secondly, the universal way of worshipping God would include all the nations or races in the world. God had chosen Israel as His people with the purpose of spreading His holiness and righteousness among other nations. The LORD God would not be the God of Israel only but He is going to be the God of all nations. God revealed His plan to prophet Isaiah, as follows:

> For I know their works and their thoughts, and I am coming to gather all nations and tongues; and they shall come and shall see my glory, and I will set a sign among them. And from them I will send survivors to the nations,...that have not heard my fame or seen my glory; and they

> shall declare my glory among the nations. And they shall bring all your brethren from all the nations as an offering to the LORD ... to my holy mountain Jerusalem, says the LORD, just as the Israelites bring their cereal offering in a clean vessel to the house of the LORD. And some of them also I will take for priests and for Levites, says the LORD. For as the new heaven and the new earth which I will make shall remain before me, says the LORD; so shall your descendants and your name remain. From new moon to new moon, and from sabbath to sabbath, all flesh shall come to worship before me, says the LORD. (Is. 66:18-23)

In these words, the LORD God declared that all nations and the tongues will praise Him everywhere and all times. God would extend the privilege to be His priests and servants to all people of the earth. This privilege will be universal.

God repeated His promise about the universal form of worship, through other prophets. God said through prophet Malachi these words:

> For from the rising of the sun to its setting my name is great among the nations, and in every place incense is offered to my name, and a pure offering; for my name is great among the nations, says the LORD of hosts. (Mal. 1:11)

God re-affirmed His promise through prophet Zephaniah (Zep. 2:11). Jesus Christ confirmed the idea of the universal form of worshipping God the Father, when he said to the Samaritan woman:

> the hour is coming, and now is, when the true worshippers will worship the Father in spirit and truth. (Jn 4:23)

Thirdly, the universal form of worshipping God would be personalized. Each believer will be led by and filled with the spirit of God. He or she would be a temple of God. St. Paul wrote to the Corinthians concerning this spiritual mystery, in the following words:

> Do you not know that you are God's temple and that God's Spirit dwells in you? If any one destroys God's temple, God will destroy him.. For God's temple is holy, and that temple you are. (I Cor. 3:16-17)

As believers are the temple of God, they are exhorted to walk in holiness and in truthfulness. St. Paul wrote to the Corinthians:

> But he who is united to the Lord becomes one spirit with him. Shun immorality. Every other sin which a man commits is outside the body; but the immoral man sins against his own body. Do you not know that your body is a temple of the Holy Spirit within you, which you have from God? You are not your own; you were bought with a price. So glorify God in your body. (I Cor. 6:17-20)

He again wrote to them, exhorting them to lead a holy life, in the following words:

> Do not be mismated with unbelievers. For what partnership have righteousness and iniquity? Or what fellowship has light with darkness? What accord has Christ with Belial? Or what has a believer in common with an unbeliever? What agreement has the temple of God with idols? For we are the temple of the living God; as God said, 'I will live in them and move among them, and I will be their God, and they shall be my people. Therefore come out from them, and be separate from them, says the Lord and touch nothing unclean; then I will welcome you, and I will a father to you, and you shall be my sons and daughters, says the Lord Almighty.' (II Cor. 6:14-18)

Fourthly, the prophesy of Jesus Christ that the true worshippers would worship God the Father in spirit and truth has to be understood with reference to Jesus Christ. This new way of worshipping was re-opened by Jesus Christ. This way is free from locations of temples. It may be free from formality of worshipping God. But it would not mean to be a vague inward spirituality. It would mean to worship in the spirit of Jesus Christ; it would mean to gather in the name of Jesus Christ (Mt. 18:20; I Cor. 1:2; 5:4); it would further mean that it would have bounds set by the word of God, the Bible (Acts 2:38-42); and it would mean to worship God in the name of Jesus Christ alone and be away from the false Christs (Mt.24:4-5; Mk 13:6; Lk. 21:8). In other words, this universal way of worship is particularized in the person of Jesus Christ. Apostle John stated in this regard, as follows:

> And this is his commandment, that we should believe in the name of his Son Jesus Christ and love one another, just as he has commanded us. All who keep his commandments abide in him, and he in them. And by this we know that he abides in us, by the Spirit which he has given us. (I Jn 3:23-24)

Conclusion

Jesus Christ prophesied a new way of worshipping God, in his conversation with the Samaritan woman. This way is a universal way. God will be worshipped in spirit and truth everywhere and by the people of the world. Each believer would be the temple of God and each believer has to walk in holiness and truth to keep God's temple holy. This universal way is not going to be a vague inward spiritual way. But it is particularized in the person of Jesus Christ; it is limited by the Bible; and the worship is to be done in the name of Jesus Christ. This universal way is personalized and particularized.

Recommended Hymns from the Methodist Hymnal

289 'Spirit divine attend our prayers'

300 Breathe on me, Breath of God;'

681 'God of mercy, God of grace,'

684 'Jesus, stand among us'

Recommended Responsive from *A Worship Manual for Scriptural or Methodist Order of Service*

107 (pp.248-249).

Endnote

 [1] Paul Lee Tan, *Encyclopedia of 7700 Illustrations: Signs of the Time*, #2617, 2619, 2620, 2621.

Chapter 11

'Righteous and Sinless Life as the Condition to Inherit the Kingdom of God,' 'Righteousness as Admission Card for the Kingdom of God,' 'Scriptural Holiness.'

Scripture

I Corinthians 6:9-20

Genesis 4:1-2

Exodus 20:3-5, 15, 17

Leviticus 18:22; 19:11

Deuteronomy 4:15-19; 5:19

Isaiah 5: 11-12

Ezekiel 3:18; 18:21-23; 33:19

John 2:1-2, 11

Romans 1:26-27; 6:10-11

Ephesians 4:12-24; 5:15-18

I John 3:4-10

Text: I Corinthians 6:9-10

A Few Versions of the Text, I Corinthians 6: 9-10

Do you not know that the unrighteous will not inherit the kingdom of God? Do not be deceived. Neither fornicators, nor idolaters, nor adulterers, nor homosexuals, nor sodomites, nor thieves, nor covetous, nor drunkards, nor revilers, nor extortioners will inherit the kingdom of God. *New King James Version*

Know ye not that the unjust shall not inherit the kingdom of God? Do not be deceived: neither fornicators, nor idolaters, nor adulterers, nor the effeminate, nor sodomites, Nor thieves, nor the covetous, nor revilers, nor rapacious, shall inherit the kingdom of God. *Explanatory Notes Upon the New Testament*

Do you not know that the unrighteous will not inherit the kingdom of God? Do not be deceived; neither the immoral, nor idolaters, nor adulterers, not sexual perverts, nor thieves, nor the greedy, nor drunkards, nor revilers, nor robbers will inherit the kingdom of God. *Revised Standard Version*

Do you not know that the wicked will not inherit the kingdom of God? Do not be deceived. Neither the sexually immoral nor idolaters nor adulterers nor male prostitutes nor homosexual offenders nor thieves nor the greedy nor drunkards nor slanderers nor swindlers will inherit the kingdom of God. *New International Version*

Surely you know that the unjust will never come into possession of the kingdom of God. Make no mistake: no fornicator or idolater, none who are guilty either of adultery or of homosexual perversion, no thieves or grabbers or drunkards or slanderers, or swindlers will inherit the kingdom of God. *The New English Bible*

Don't you know that those doing such things have no share in the Kingdom of God? Don't fool yourselves. Those who live immoral lives, who are idol worshippers, adulterer or homosexuals, will have no share in the kingdom of God. Neither will thieves or greedy people, drunkards, slanderers, or robbers. *The Living Bible Illustrated*

Don't you know that wicked people won't inherit the kingdom of God? Stop deceiving yourselves! People who continue to commit sexual sins, who worship false gods, those who commit adultery, homosexuals, or thieves, those who are greedy or drunk, who use abusive language, or who rob people will inherit the kingdom of God. *God's Word*

Introduction

CHML is a radio station in Hamilton, Ontario, Canada. On February 14, 1995, a host of talk show of the radio station mentioned that there is a church in California, U. S. A., which has 70% homosexuals as members and which has two ministers who are homosexual and lesbian. This church ordained self-confessed practising homosexual persons about two years ago. Those ministers were not officially ordained by a bishop of the Lutheran Church. There is a trend among other denominations to ordain homosexual persons as ministers. The host of the talk show asked his radio audience to respond to the following questions: Will they approve the ordination of homosexual ministers? And how would they respond to the ministry of those ordained ministers? In response to these questions, a listener quoted the verses from I Corinthians 6:9-10:

> Do you not know that the unrighteous will not inherit the kingdom of God? Do not be deceived; neither the immoral, nor idolaters, nor adulterers, nor sexual perverts, nor thieves, nor the greedy, nor drunkards, nor revilers, nor robbers will inherit the kingdom of God.

The listener, who was a lady, made it quite clear that homosexuality is sinful and the homosexuals should not be ordained as ministers by a church.

The Church of Jesus Christ stands for sanctity of a married couple, a husband and a wife. Homosexuality is a deviant form of relationship; it is a sin in the sight of God. To ordain homosexuals is a serious breach of the high calling of God; it is a form of deliberate deception.

The God of the Bible is the most holy God who asked His people or believers to be holy as He is holy. Apostle Peter wrote to Christians the following words:

> As obedient children, do not be conformed to the passions of your former ignorance, but as he who called you is holy, be holy yourselves in all your conduct; since it is written, 'You shall be holy, for I am holy'.
> (I Pet. 1:14-16)

The gospel, the good news, is for the sinner to give up sins and to lead holy and righteous life, befitting to the children of the holy God. The great commission of the Church is to preach the righteousness of God in all parts of the world. This is the special commission of the Methodist Church. This commission is mentioned in the "Public Reception Service for Christians," wishing to be Methodists:

> Within the Christian Church-One, Holy, Catholic, and Apostolic- the Methodist Church holds and cherished a true place, having been raised up by God to spread Scriptural Holiness throughout the world.[1]

These words tell us and remind us that the Methodist Church was raised by God for the purpose of spreading a scriptural holiness throughout the world; therefore, the Methodist Church has a very specified mission among all other Protestant and evangelical denominations.

The Reverend John Wesley (A. D. 1703-1791) was a founder of Methodist Church. He often spoke of Methodism as a scriptural Christianity; or Methodism as a Protestant Church, which based its theology on the word of God. As Methodism was a scriptural Christianity to Rev. John Wesley, he specified the universal mission of Methodism in terms of spreading Scriptural Holiness in the world.

There are different notions of holiness because there are different religions in the world. Rev. John Wesley limited his thinking of holiness to the Bible only. In his writings, he attempted to define holiness in a variety of concepts.

(a) He defined a scriptural holiness as image of God,[2] the image of God stamped on the heart,[3] the life of God in the soul of man.[4]

(b) Wesley defined the scriptural holiness as the mind of Christ,[5] the mind of Christ which enables us to walk as Christ walked.[6]

(c) Wesley defined it as obedience to Christ's commands and as imitation of Christ. He exhorted his followers, saying:

Show then your love to Christ by keeping his commandments, by walking in all; his ordinances blameless. Honour Christ by obeying him with all your might, by serving him with all your strength. Glorify Christ by imitating Christ in all things, by walking as he walked. Keep to Christ by keeping in all his ways.[7]

(d) John Wesley defined the scriptural holiness as the new creation, the renewal of soul in the image of God, wherein he was created.[8]

(e) Wesley also defined it as leading pure or sinless life. He wrote the following words:

I testify unto you, that if you still continue in sin, Christ shall profit you nothing; that Christ is no saviour to you, unless he saves you from your sins; and that unless it purify your heart, faith shall profit you nothing.[9]

Rev. John Wesley exhorted Christians to be zealous of good works. Why did he do so? He was critical of the heretical teaching similar to that of Simon Magus, who was a magician in Samaria and embraced Christianity and wished to buy healing power from St. Peter (Acts 8:9-24). St. Peter opposed Simon Magus at Samaria and at Rome also. He was the first heretic of all.[10] According to a church tradition, Simon Magus taught:

that Christ has done, as well as suffered all; that his righteousness being imputed to us, we need none of our own; that seeing there was so much righteousness and holiness in Him, there needs none in us; that to think we have any, or to desire or seek any, is to renounce Christ; that from the beginning to the end of salvation, all is in Christ, nothing in man; and that those who teach otherwise are legal Preachers, and nothing of the gospel.[11]

Rev. John Wesley thought of this teaching as "blow at the root of all holiness," all true religion; it leaves no place for holiness. It makes men afraid of personal holiness, afraid of cherishing any thought of it, or motion toward it, lest they should deny the faith, and reject Christ and his righteousness. The teaching makes people more afraid of "the works of God," than "the works of devil."[12] He condemned the heretical teaching of Simon Magus as the wisdom from beneath, a masterpiece of Satan. He pointed out to the people that according to the teaching of Simon Magus,

> Men are holy, without a grain of holiness in them! Holy in Christ, however unholy in themselves; they are in Christ, without one jot of the mind that was in Christ; in Christ, though their nature is whole in them. They are 'complete in him' though they are, in themselves, as proud, as vain, as covetous, as passionate as ever.[13]

Having denounced this simplistic teaching of Simon Magus, Rev. John Wesley argued with the people, on the basis of the scripture, as follows:

> "Know ye not" whoever teacheth you otherwise, "that the unrighteous shall not inherit the kingdom of God?" "Be not deceived"; although there are many lies in wait to deceive, and that under the fair pretence of exalting Christ; - a pretence which the more easily steals upon you, because "to you he is precious."[14]

Then Wesley added

> But as the Lord liveth, "neither fornicators, nor idolaters, nor adulterers, nor effeminate, nor sodomites, nor thieves, nor covetous, not drunkards, nor revilers, nor extortioners, shall inherit the kingdom of God." "Such" indeed "were some of you. But ye are washed, but ye are sanctified," as well as " justified in the name of the Lord Jesus, and by the Spirit of our God."[15]

Rev. Wesley quoted these verses from I Cor. 6:9-11.

Introduction of the Text

The verses from I Corinthians 6:9-11 ask Christians to lead a holy or sinless life in order to inherit the kingdom of God. We will concentrate on a few verses from this section, namely, as follow

> **Do you not know that the unrighteous will not inherit the kingdom of God? Do not be deceived; neither the immoral, nor idolaters,**

nor adulterers, nor sexual perverts, nor thieves, nor the greedy, nor drunkards, nor revilers, nor robbers will inherit the kingdom of God.
(I Corinthians 6: 9-10)

This is the text of our meditation now.

The Context of the Text

Apostle Paul wrote the words of the text to the Corinthians because he came to know that there was a member of the church at Corinth who was living with his father's wife (I Cor. 5:1). This act of cohabitation was a worse sin; therefore, St. Paul advised the church to remove him from the congregation. Christians should not encourage such a sinful lifestyle and they should dissociate themselves from such a man. St. Paul wrote to the Corinthians:

> But rather I wrote to you not to associate with any one who bears the name of brother if he is guilty of immorality or greed, or is an idolater, reviler, drunkard, or robber - not even to eat with such a one. (I Cor. 5:11)

St. Paul emphasized the same idea when he wrote the words of the text of our meditation:

> Do you not know that the unrighteous will not inherit the kingdom of God? Do not be deceived; neither the immoral, nor idolaters, nor adulterers, not sexual perverts, nor thieves, nor the greedy, nor drunkards, nor revilers, nor robbers will inherit the kingdom of God. (I Corinthians 6:9-10)

This is the text, within its historical setting.

An Analysis of the Text

This text has two ideas. (A) The first idea is a question, apostle Paul asked to the Corinthians, whether they know that the unrighteous would not inherit the kingdom of God.

(B) The second idea is the warning of being deceived that all sinners would inherit the kingdom of God. The immoral, idolaters, adulterers, sexual pervert, thieves, greedy, drunkards, revilers, and robbers would not inherit the kingdom of God.

An Exposition of Ideas

(A) The first idea of the text is a question, apostle Paul asked to the Corinthians, whether they know that the unrighteous would not inherit the kingdom of God. The answer to this question is that the unrighteous would not inherit the kingdom of God; because all kinds of sins are incompatible with the kingdom of God. God is holy, pure, and righteous God. Man's sins, his unholiness, unrighteousness are opposite of God's characteristics. God accepts man when he is purified, sanctified, and justified or made fit to be in fellowship with God. St. Paul reminded the previous spiritual condition of the Corinthians, before they became Christians. Corinthians were Gentiles, now knowing the true God and His righteousness. They were idol worshippers; they were stealing and robbing the things of others. They were drinking heavily. They were practising adultery. When they heard the gospel of Jesus Christ, their sins were forgiven and they were changed by the work of the Holy Spirit in them. They gave up their formal immoral life and began to live a life led by the Spirit of God in Jesus Christ. Concerning these two phases of life, St. Paul wrote to the Corinthians:

> And such were some of you. But you were washed, you were sanctified, you were justified in the name of the Lord Jesus Christ and in the Spirit of our God. (I Cor. 6:11)

In other words, the Corinthians were cleansed by God in the name of Jesus Christ from their former sins; they were made holy, just and acceptable to God. God adopted them as His children.

St. Paul exhorted the Ephesians with reference to a similar situation, saying:

> Now this I affirm and testify in the Lord, that you must no longer live as the Gentiles do, in the futility of their minds; they are darkened in their understanding, alienated from the life of God because of the ignorance that is in them, due to their hardness of heart; they have become callous and have given themselves up to licentiousness, greedy to practice every kind of uncleanness. You did not so learn Christ! - assuming that you heard about him and were taught in him, as the truth is in Jesus. Put off your old nature which belongs to your former manner of life and is corrupt through deceitful lusts, and be renewed in the spirit of your

minds, and put on the new nature, created after the likeness of God in true righteousness and holiness. (Eph. 4:17-24 cf. Rom. 6:10-11)

Apostle John, like St. Paul, wrote to Christians about the similar spiritual matter, saying:

> Every one who commits sin is guilty of lawlessness; sin is lawlessness. You know that he [Jesus Christ] appeared to take away sins, and in him there is no sin. No one who abides in him sins; no one who sins has either seen him or known him. Little children, let no one deceive you. He who does right is righteous, as he is righteous. He who commits sin is of the devil; for the devil has sinned from the beginning. The reason the Son of God appeared was to destroy the works of the devil. No one born of God commits sin; for God's nature abides in him, and he cannot sin because he is born of God. By this it may be seen who are the children of God, and who are the children of the devil; whoever does not do right is not of God, nor he who does not love his brother. (I Jn 3:4-10)

The apostles exhorted Christians to lead holy and righteous life; because without this changed life, they would be not admitted into the kingdom of God.

(B) The second idea of the text is the warning of being deceived that all sinners would inherit the kingdom of God. The immoral, idolaters, adulterers, sexual pervert, thieves, greedy, drunkards, revilers, and robbers would not inherit the kingdom of God. We will attempt to state biblical positions on these various types of sinners.

(a) An immoral person is the person who acts against the commandments of the holy God. His acts and desires are sinful; they are against the righteous and holy will of God. An immoral person is also called "a wicked or unrighteous man." The righteous God judges the wicked and punishes him for his sins (Job 20:27-29; Ps. 9:5-6, 17; Pr.11:21; Is. 11:4; Ezek. 3:18). The wicked has to turn away from his wickedness and ask God for His forgiveness and God would be delighted to save him (Ezek. 18:21-23; 33:19).

(b) An idolater is a person who worship idols and images made out of metal, stone, and wood. Idol worship implies that the honour and praise of the true and living God is given to other gods, who are the creatures, and cannot have life in them. The LORD God asked the people of Israel to worship Him alone; and they were prohibited to make an image of anything and to bow down before other gods. God would punish those who break His command (Ex. 20:3-5; Lev. 19:4; 26:1; Deut. 4:15-19; 5:8; 27:15; Ps. 97:7; Is. 2:20).

(c) An adulterer is a person who commits adultery with his or her neighbour. Committing an adultery is a sin against the sanctity of marriage between a man and a woman (Gen. 2:18, 23-24; 3:1; I Cor. 7:2-5; Heb. 13:4; Pr. 18:22; I Tim. 3:12) as they become one flesh (Gen. 2:24; Mt. 5:32; Mk 10:9; Rom. 7:2). Adultery was a serious sin, punishable by death penalty (Lev. 18:20; 20:10; Ex. 20:14; Deut. 5:18).

(d) A sexual pervert is homosexual man and lesbian woman. These forms of unnatural sexual relationship are the deviated sexual practices. The primary purpose of holy matrimony is to procreate the human race (Gen. 4:1-2; 33:5; Jn 2:1-2, 11). The perverted forms of sexual relationship are against the will of God (Lev. 18:22; 20:13; Rom. 1:26-27; I Cor. 6:9-10). The sinners, who commit this type of sins, should change themselves in order to enter the kingdom of God, as every other sinner is expected to do the same.

(e) Thieves and robbers are the persons who take away the possessions of others by deception and force. The acts of thefts and robbery are serious sins in the sight of God. The LORD God commanded His people not to steal (Ex. 20:15; Lev. 19:11; Deut. 5:19).

(f) A greedy person is a person who is not satisfied with what he has obtained, therefore, he wants to covet the things of others by immoral means. The LORD God commanded His people not to covet any thing of their neighbours (Ex. 20:17; Deut. 5:21; Rom. 7:7). Greed for power and wealth is a root of all evils (I Tim.6:10). It is a mother of sins. It is against the will of God.

(h) A drunkard is a person who enjoys hard liquor all times and who loses his reasoning and moral capacity to say and do right things.

The Bible lists the evil effects of strong drink, such as: becoming unconscious of shame and decency (Gen. 9:21); loss of proper sense (Gen. 27:27; I Sam. 25:36) inability to distinguish between sacred and profane (Lev. 10:9-10); loss of understanding in general (Hos. 4:11); inability to distinguish between right and wrong (Gen. 1: 33-34) having no regard for God's deeds (Is. 5:11-12); corrupt behaviour (Am. 2:8), etc. For these reasons, the Bible prohibits drinking strong drinks in case of the persons who administer justice and who render religious service (Lev. 10:9-10; Pr. 31:4-5; Ezek. 44:21). Apostles of the early church exhorted Christians not to drink (Rom. 14:21; Eph. 5:15-18).

The people who continue in these types of sins would not inherit the kingdom of God. All these sins are against the body of Jesus Christ, the Church. St. Paul told this truth to the Corinthians, in these plain words:

> But he who is united to the Lord becomes one spirit with him. Shun immorality. Every other sin which a man commits is outside the body; but the immoral man sins against his own body. Do you not know that your body is a temple of the Holy Spirit within you, which you have from God? You are not your own; you were bought with a price. So glorify God in your body. (I Cor. 6:17-20)

In these verses, the word "body" is used as the body of believers and the body of an individual. God in Jesus Christ abides in the body of an individual and in the congregation of the believers. Both bodies are sanctified by the presence of Jesus Christ. Therefore, there is no place for sin in those bodies.

Conclusion

Apostle Paul made very clear to the church at Corinth that the unrighteous people will not inherit the kingdom of God. He identified those unrighteous people, such as the immoral, idolaters, adulterers, sexual perverts, thieves, etc., who would not inherit the kingdom of God. The people who are forgiven their sins and who are sanctified by the Spirit of the Lord Jesus Christ and who are leading holy and righteous life would inherit the kingdom. The Christian denominations should know this and thereby they make their church policies about ordaining ministers to preach the gospel of holiness and righteousness. Methodist Church has a special role in the ministry.

Recommended Hymns from the Methodist Hymnal

400 'Take my life, and let it be'

547 'The things my God doth hate'

550 'O for a heart to praise my God,'

557 'What is our calling's glorious hope'

Recommended Responsive Reading form *A Worship Manual for Scriptural or Methodist Order of Service*

89 (pp. 211-213).

Endnotes

[1] *The Book of Offices,* (London: The Methodist Publishing House, 1936), p. 48.

[2] *The Works of John Wesley*, (Grand Rapids, Michigan: Baker Book House, 3rd ed., 1984), Vol. X, p. 203.

[3] Ibid., Vol. III, p. 341.

[4] Ibid., Vol. III, p. 341.

[5] Ibid., Vol. X, p. 203.

[6] Ibid., Vol. III, p. 431; Vol. VII, p. 316.

[7] *The Works of John Wesley*, Vol. X, p. 369.

[8] Ibid., Vol. VII, p. 316.

[9] Ibid., Vol. X, p. 367.

[10] Henry Chawdwick, *The Early Church*, (Harmondsworth, England: Penguin Books Ltd., Reprinted 1974), p.82.

[11] *The Works of John Wesley*, Vol. X, p. 366.

[12] Ibid., Vol. X, pp. 366-367.

[13] *The Works of John Wesley*, Vol. X, pp. 366f.

[14] Ibid., Vol. X, p. 367.

[15] Loc. cit.

Chapter 12

'A Radical Reorientation,'<br>'Difference Between Godly Grief
and Worldly Grief,'<br>'Godly Grief, the Cause of Redemptive
Repentance,'<br>'Godly Grief, a Requisite of Redemption.'

Scripture

II Corinthians 7:5-14

Genesis 25:29-34; 27:35, 46; 32:11, 14-15; 33:3, 4

Exodus 14:16-17,28

Proverbs 28:14; 29:1

Matthew 23:3-4

Luke 15:18-19; 19:5, 8-10

Romans 2:5

II Corinthians 2:1, 3-11, 7:9f.; 11:22f.; 12:14; 13:1f.

Hebrews 3:12-13

Text: II Corinthians 7:10

A Few Versions of the Text II Corinthians 7:10

For godly sorrow produces a repentance leading to salvation, not to be regretted; but the sorrow of the world produces death. *New King James Version*

For godly sorrow worketh repentance unto salvation not to be repented of: whereas the sorrow of the world worketh death. *Explanatory Notes Upon the New Testament*

For godly grief produces a repentance that leads to salvation and bring no regret, but worldly grief produces death. *Revised Standard Version*

Godly sorrow brings repentance that leads to salvation and leaves no regret, but worldly sorrow brings death. *New International Version*

From the wound which is borne in God's way brings a change of heart too salutary to regret; but the hurt which is borne in the world's way brings death. *The New English Bible*

For God sometimes uses sorrow in our lives to help us turn away from sin and seek eternal life. We should never regret his sending it. But the sorrow of the man who is not a Christian is not the sorrow of true repentance and does not prevent eternal death. *The Living Bible Illustrated*

In fact, to be distressed in a godly way causes people to change the way they think and act and leads them to be saved. No one can regret that. But the distress that the world causes brings only death. *God's Word*

Introduction

(1) Canadian society seems to be confused over the issue how to treat dangerous criminals. The society cares more for the rights of criminals than the rights of victims. Victims have to fight for their rights more than the criminals do. The parole board of the federal government is anxious to release dangerous criminals from prison. The parole board

always argues that the criminals have paid enough for their crimes; the criminals have suffered more than they deserved; the criminals are sorry for what damage and pain they caused for others; they should be shown mercy and given another chance to be in the society; they should be given another opportunity to be rehabilitated. The society is kept in darkness about where those criminals would be resettled. When those criminals are released from prison, within a short time, they do similar dangerous crimes. We have such examples. When Jonathan Yeo was released, he killed Nina DeVilliers on August 9, 1991. When Donaldson was released, he raped and killed Christopher Stevenson in Brampton in 1989. These facts confirm the fact that the repeat offenders have not changed their hearts. Therefore, they commit the similar crimes. The parole board cannot understand a distinction between regret and true repentance. The criminals regret offences because they found guilty of the crimes; and they had to lose their freedom and enjoyment of life. Jonathan Yoho committed suicide because he regretted for being chased by police officers as he was a suspect.

(2) A murder was sentenced to death. The murder had a brother. The State was deeply indebted to his brother for his excellent service to society. His brother approached the governor of the State and obtained a paper for his brother's pardon. The man went to visit his brother in the prison, with the pardon paper in his pocket. He asked his brother, 'What would you do if you received a pardon?' The criminal replied, 'The first thing I would do is to track down the judge who sentenced me, and murder him; and the next thing I would do is to track down the chief witness, and murder him.' The brother of the criminal found that his brother did not repent and he was planning to take revenge. Therefore, he went back with the pardon paper in his pocket.[1]

This event teaches us that if there in no true repentance, there should be no pardon.

(3) In the Imperial Gallery in Vienna, there is a picture drawn by Ruben, depicting that Emperor was refused admission into the church by St. Ambrose (A. D. 340-397). The picture was based on the event

as follows. The Emperor Theodosius (ca. A. D.346-395) killed 1,500 citizens of Thessalonica in A. D. 390. The church placed the Emperor under the ban. The Emperor Theodosius wanted to enter the cathedral in Milan. When he proceeded to enter the Cathedral, he was arrested at the portal by the intrepid Bishop Ambrose, who forbade him entrance until he had done public penance for his crime. The Emperor argued saying, if he had been guilty of homicide, so had king David, the man after God's own heart. St. Ambrose sternly replied, "You have imitated David in his crime, imitate him in repentance."

This picture stands for the principles of power of moral indignation and of necessity of repentance before forgiveness can be granted.[2]

Introduction of the Text

The aforesaid illustrations teach us the necessity of repentance, because it leads to the spiritual salvation and makes the repentant useful for society. This spiritual fact is affirmed by the words of St. Paul when he wrote to the Corinthians as follows:

> **For godly grief produces a repentance that leads to salvation and bring no regret, but worldly grief produces death.** (II Cor. 7:10)

This is the text of our meditation now.

The Context of the Text

When St. Paul wrote his first letter to the Corinthians in A. D. 55, some leaders of the local church at Corinth did not like the letter and they rebelled against St. Paul. That rebellion was led by some Jewish Christians (II Cor. 11:22f.), who called themselves 'apostles.' Those apostles created the disturbance in the church at Corinth. Therefore, St. Paul had to come hurriedly from Ephesus to Corinth to calm down the rebellion and disturbance (II Cor. 2:1; 12:14; 13:1f.). But his visit proved painful (II Cor. 2:1), and he had to go back to Ephesus, without quelling the revolt. When he returned to Ephesus, he was determined to calm down the revolt. Therefore, he wrote another severe letter, ordering the Corinthians to mend their ways and to punish the rebels

(II Cor. 2:3-4, 9). He took a firm stand against the rebels. His blunt writing shocked them; they were made aware of their faults. His letter deeply grieved the Corinthians. Many of them took courage to correct the situation. After the letter, St. Paul sent Titus to Corinth to see whether the situation was changed. Titus brought the news from Corinth that the situation had improved immensely; the Corinthians had punished the rebellious ringleader (II Cor. 2:5-11) and the rebellion was turned into 'godly grief' (II Cor. 7:9f.). St. Paul's letter made the Corinthians to repent or to mend their ways. His letter acted like a bitter medicine, e. g. quinine, which makes a patient free from fever and disease. Christian leaders have to take a firm stand against wickedness in order to improve the spiritual condition of churches.

An Analysis of the Text

In this text, St. Paul spoke about two types of grief and their results. (A) The first idea is that the godly grief produces repentance. This type of repentance positively brings forth two results. (i) The first result is that the repentance leads to salvation. (ii) The second result is that the repentance brings no regret for the change.

(B) The second idea is that the worldly grief produces death. The worldly grief negatively brings forth two results, leading to death (i) The first negative result is that it does not leads to salvation. (ii) The second negative result is that it does not produce a change in man.

An Exposition of the Ideas

(A) The first idea of the text is that the godly grief produces repentance. This type of repentance positively brings forth two results. (i) The first result is that the repentance leads to salvation. (ii) The second result is that the repentance brings no regret for the change.

The godly grief or sorrow is the true repentance. It is not just a verbal expression such as 'I am sorry,' and no change in conduct. The godly grief makes man to realize the effects of his sinful acts upon his own life and upon the life of others; he realizes that his evil actions hurt the feelings of others. He sees the necessity to change his life from being sinful and harmful to being good and helpful to others. He wishes to be good and right with himself and with others; he wishes to be a child of God. He attempts to bring this desired change in himself.

Jesus Christ made a parable around these spiritual ideas. The parable is popularly known as the parable of the prodigal son. In this parable, the youngest son decided to go away from his father's house, with his share of the property. He spent his riches on the enjoyment of life. He became poor and he cannot afford to eat. He was sent to look after pigs. He was eating what the pigs were eating. It was a most humiliating experience to a Jewish young man. While he was in that deplorable condition, he recalled how happy he was in his father's home; he realized that he lost good food, good clothes, and an affectionate family, because he acted stupidly and selfishly. He realized that he did wrong to his caring father; and he sinned against God by his sins. He decided to return to his father's home and expressed his repentance to his father. He made up his mind as to what he appropriately should say to his father upon his return. He said to himself:

> I will arise and go to my father, and I will say to him, 'Father, I have sinned against heaven and before you; I am no longer worthy to be called your son; treat me as one of your hired servants.' (Lk. 15:18-19)

The prodigal son was truly repentant because his grief was godly. He became humble and repentant. He was a changed man. His father accepted him because of his change of heart. His father restored him to the status of his sons. His return to his father's home brought joy to his father and relief from wants to himself. He became a happy man, abiding with his father. He never repented of this spiritual change in himself.

The intention of the parable was to teach people how God forgives sins of man, who repents, and He gives joy of salvation to man. Jesus Christ did not only teach this noble spiritual idea to the people but also he demonstrated godly love by his association with sinners and publicans. There are a few events about this. A typical event is given how Zacchaeus responded to Jesus Christ. Zacchaeus was a tax collector, a sinner. He became rich because he cheated many. He was a chief tax collector. He heard much about Jesus Christ. He wished to see Jesus from a distance. As he was short, he would be unable to see Jesus in a crowd. Therefore, he climbed up on a sycamore tree to see Jesus passing by or under. When Jesus Christ saw Zacchaeus, Jesus said to him, "Zacchaeus, make haste and come down; for I must stay at your home today." (Lk. 19:5) Zecchaeus came down from the tree and received Jesus surprisingly and cheerfully. While he was taking Jesus to his home, he said to Jesus Christ:

> Behold, Lord, the half of my goods I give to the poor; and if I have defrauded any one of anything I restore fourfold. (Lk. 19:8)

Zecchaeus said so to Jesus Christ, because he realized the wrongs he did to others; he wanted to recompense others fourfold and to do charitable things for the poor. He was a changed person from within. When Jesus Christ heard Zacchaeus' righteous desire, he said to him:

> Today salvation has come to this house, since he also is a son of Abraham. For the Son of man came to seek and to save the lost. (Lk. 19:9-10)

Zacchaeus became a saved child of God. He and his family were saved. He never regretted this positive change in his life.

In the Old Testament, there is a similar event how two brothers were reconciled, because of the change of their heart. Jacob and Esau were brothers. Jacob was the younger brother, who cheated his eldest brother Esau on two separate occasions. (1) First, Jacob gave his brother Esau bread and pottage of lentils, when he was very hungry and bought his brother's birthright in return (Gen. 25:29-34). This was a cheap bargain or an act of cheating. (2) Secondly, Isaac, their father, wished to bless Esau before his death, and he asked Esau to prepare food for him. When Esau went hunting, their mother Rebekah, told Jacob to serve food to his father before Esau returned from hunting. Jacob pretended to be Esau and obtained his father's blessings, which should had been bestowed on Esau. When Esau returned from hunting and prepared food for their father and went to receive his father's blessings, Isaac told Esau, 'Your brother came with guile, and he has taken away your blessing.' (Gen. 27:35). Esau was very angry at his brother; he wanted to kill Jacob for cheating him. Jacob's mother Rebekah asked Jacob to go to Haran till Esau forgets what Jacob did to him. (Gen. 27:46)

Jacob returned after twenty-five years. He was still afraid of Esau that he would kill him (Gen. 32:11). Jacob was ready to pay for the damage he did to Esau. He wanted to appease him and to be reconciled with him. He sent 200 she-goats, 20 he-goats, 40 cows, and many other animals (Gen. 32:14-15) for compensations. When Jacob saw his brother Esau approaching him, Jacob humbled himself and bowed to the ground seven times in the presence of his brother (Gen. 33:3). Esau was fully convinced of Jacob's desire to be reconciled. Esau ran to meet Jacob, and embraced him, fell on his neck and kissed him, and they both wept (Gen. 33:4). Jacob was a changed person when he returned to see his brother Esau. He never regretted being reconciled with his brother.

How the godly grief produces redemptive repentance is illustrated by the life of St. Augustine (A. D. 354-430). Augustine was a heavy drinker; he was a chain smoker; he was a professional gambler. He had many sexual affairs with women; he was an evil man. But his mother used to pray for her son that God may change him and use him for the kingdom of God. Augustine repented of his sins and became a saved man by God's grace. He went to a seminary and became a priest. Because of his long service to humanity, he was recognized as a Christian saint.

(B) The second idea of the text is that the worldly grief produces death. The worldly grief negatively brings forth two results, leading to death. (i) The first negative result is that it does not leads to salvation. (ii) The second negative result is that it does not produce a change in man.

The first negative result of the worldly grief is that it does not lead to salvation. Salvation is opposite of death. A prerequisite of salvation is an acknowledgement of wrong doings or sins, and subsequent repentance for the wrong doings.

The worldly grief does not produce repentance, because it fails to see the God who forgives sins. On the other hand, the worldly grief makes a person stubborn or hard hearted. It causes a person to act like Pharaoh of Egypt, Ramses II (1301-1234 B. C.). The heart of Pharaoh was hardened against the demand of God through Moses; he was not willing to see the hand of God behind those plagues; he was not willing to humble before God (Ex. 14:16,17, 28). As his heart was hardened, he caused death of his people and the army.

The writer of the Book of Proverbs generalizes about this spiritual matter, saying:

> Blessed is the man who fears the LORD always; but he who hardens his heart will fall into calamity. (Pr. 28:14, cf. Pr. 29:1)

St. Paul, in conformity with the idea, wrote to the Romans, in the following words:

> But by your hard and impenitent heart you are storing up wrath for yourself on the day of wrath when God's righteous judgement will be revealed. (Rom. 2:5)

St. Paul wanted the Romans to be repentant in order to be saved from the wrath of God. In his Letter to the Hebrews, he exhorted the believers not to harden their hearts, in these words:

> Take care, brethren, lest there be in any of you an evil, unbelieving heart, leading you away from the living God. But exhort one another every day, as long as it is called 'today', that none of you be hardened by the deceitfulness of sin. (Heb. 3:12-13)

(ii) The second negative result is that the worldly grief does not produce a change in man. As the worldly grief does not create a change in the heart of a person, it causes the person to kill himself spiritually and physically. This actuality is demonstrated by the suicide of Judas Iscariot, who was a disciple of Jesus Christ. He betrayed Jesus Christ and delivered him to be tried by the religious and state authority. He learned that Jesus was to be crucified; then he felt a deepest regret for his action. He wished to undo his action. He went to the chief priest and elders and said to them, "I have sinned in betraying innocent blood." (Mt. 23:3-4) He realized that he committed a sin against man and God. He could not face the results of his evil deed. He was so much guilt ridden that he committed suicide. He did not repent for his sin, believing in God that He could forgive his sin. He finally took his life.

How the worldly grief produces death is illustrated by the life of Adolf Hitler (A. D. 1889-1945). Hitler became a dictator of Germany. He ordered to exterminate chronically insane and incurable 70,000 Germans in 'euthanasia centres.' These centres were then used for insane cases from concentration camps. He ordered to kill six million Jews who were in the concentration camps. He killed many innocent people. Germany was defeated in the second world war (September 1, 1939- September 2, 1945). He had many regrets during his last days. Hitler committed suicide on 30 April 1945,[3] because he had no courage to face results of his wicked deeds.

Conclusion

We know that we are sinful by nature. No one is righteous before the most holy and righteous God. We must believe in the grace o God, manifested in Jesus Christ. By the grace of God, we all shall be saved. But we have to repent for our sins before God pardons our offences and sins. God does not delight in the death of a sinner but He delights saving the sinners.

Without the godly and redemptive grief, we shall be spiritually deemed to die. Let us have that godly grief in our hearts. Then God can save us from the spiritual decay and destruction. Let us repent and be saved.

Recommended Hymns from the Methodist Hymna

7 'O Heavenly King, look down from above;'

351 'I hear Thy welcome voice'

353 'Just as I am, without one plea'

373 'Lord, I was blind! I could not see'

498 'Rock of Ages, cleft for me,'

669 'Dear Lord and Father of mankind,'

Recommended Responsive Reading from the Methodist Hymnal
44 (p. 402),

Recommended Responsive Reading from *A Worship Manual for Scriptural or Methodist Order of Service*
38 (pp. 131-132).

[1] Paul Lee Tan, *Encyclopedia of 7700 Illustrations: Signs of the Time*, #4978.

[2] Paul Lee Tan, op. cit., # 4982.

[3] Paul Johnson, *A History of the Modern World from 1917 to the 1990s*, (London: Weidenfeld and Nicolson, Revised Ed., 1991), p.413.

Chapter 13

'The Ultimate Goal for the Believers,' 'Straightforward Spiritual Race of the Believers,' 'The Way to be Spiritually Winners.' 'Giving up of Prestigious Things for Christ Jesus'

Scripture

Philippians 3:1-21

Genesis 17:10-14, 25; 29:18-20, 30; 32:38; 35:16-18

Leviticus 12:3

Deuteronomy 5:32-33

Joshua 1:6-7

I Samuel 9:2

I Kings 12:21

Ezra 4:1

Proverbs 4:25-27

Acts 21:40; 22:3; 23:6; 26:5

I Corinthians 9:24-25

II Corinthians 1:5; 4:10-11; 11:24-28

Galatians 2:20; 6:17

Colossians 1:24

Philippians 4:13-14

II Timothy 4:7-8

James 1:12

Text: Philippians 3:13-14

A Few Versions of the Text, Philippians 3:13-14

Brethren, I do not count myself to have apprehended; but one thing I do, forgetting those things which are behind and reaching toward to those things which are ahead. I press toward the goal for the prize of the upward call of God in Christ Jesus. *New King James Version*

Brethren, I do not count myself to have apprehended; but one thing I do, forgetting the things that are behind, and reaching forth unto the things which are before, I press toward the goal, for the prize of the high calling of God in Christ Jesus. *Explanatory Notes Upon the New Testament*

Brethren, I do not consider that I have made it my own but one thing I do, forgetting what lies behind and straining forward to what lies ahead. I press on toward the goal for the prize of the upward call of God in Christ Jesus. *Revised Standard Version*

Brothers, I do not consider myself yet to have taken hold of it. But one thing I do: Forgetting what is behind and straining toward what is ahead, I press on toward the goal to win the prize for which God has called me heavenward in Christ Jesus. *New International Version*

My friends, I do not reckon myself to have got hold of it yet. All I can say is this: forgetting what is behind me, and reaching out for that which lies ahead, I press towards the goal to win the prize which is God's call to the life above, in Christ Jesus. *The New English Bible*

No, dear brothers, I am still not all I should be but I am bringing all my energies to bear on this one thing: Forgetting the past and looking forward to what lies ahead. I strain to reach the end of the race and receive the prize for which God is calling us up to heaven because of what Christ Jesus did for us. *The Living Bible Illustrated.*

Brothers and sisters, I can't consider myself a winner yet. This is what I do: I do not look back, I lengthen my stride, and I run straight toward the goal to win the prize that God's heavenly call offers in Christ Jesus. *God's Word*

Introduction

(1) Greeks had started Olympic games as a national festival since 776 B. C. in honour of Zeus.[1] Every four years those games take place in the large cities of the world. In order to participate in the Olympic games, athletes have to train themselves vigorously; they have to exercise and practice every day for many years. By training and hard work, the athletes make themselves physically and mentally qualified for the competition. When the athletes win the race, they are awarded and honoured. By their success, the nations which they represent, are given recognition and fame. In 1996, Olympic games were held in Atlanta, Georgia. Donavan Bailey won the golden medal in the race. Canadians were happy and proud of the success of Bailey.

(2) There are stories about the athletes how they won or lost the race. In the ancient time, there was a well-known runner; he was the fastest runner and there was no one to win against him in a race. His opponent thought of a trick to lower the speed of the fasted runner. He put a few gold plated balls in his pouch. As the race started, he started to throw those balls, one after another. The fastest runner was tempted to pick up those balls. As he used to stop in order to pick the balls, he was losing time and his opponent was going ahead of him. The fasted runner lost the race against his opponent. This story has a

moral lesson such as when an individual loses the straight way to his goal by temptation he loses the race; or the runner has to concentrate on his goal by avoiding temptations.

Introduction of the Text

St. Paul had seen how athletes train themselves in order to participate in race and how they motivate themselves to win the prize against other participants. He wished that the believers should learn from the successful athletes in order to be successful in their spiritual race. He had exhorted the believers in various churches to run the spiritual race as athletes. He wrote to the Christians at Corinth:

> Do you not know that in a race all the runners compete, but only one receives the prize? So run that you may obtain it. Every athlete exercises self-control in all things. They do it to receive a perishable wreath, but we an imperishable. (I Cor. 9:24-25)

St. Paul compared his mission to be faithful to the faith in Jesus Christ with running a race; he was hoping to be rewarded for running the race successfully. He wrote to Timothy about the conviction in the following words:

> I have fought the good fight, I have finished the race, I have kept the faith. Henceforth there is laid up for me the crown of righteousness, which the Lord, the righteous judge, will award to me on the Day, and not only to me but also to all who have loved his appearing. (II Tim. 4:7-8)

In these words, St. Paul encouraged Timothy to keep the faith in the face of crises.

St. Paul was anticipating a spiritual award at the hands of Jesus Christ; he wished other believers to follow him in their spiritual race. He wrote to the believers at Philippi:

> **Brethren, I do not consider that I have made it my own but one thing I do, forgetting what lies behind and straining forward to what lies ahead. I press on toward the goal for the prize of the upward call of God in Christ Jesus.** (Philippians 3:13-14)

This is the text of our meditation now.

The Context of the Text

St. Paul had to exhort the church at Philippi, asking them to forget the past glorious things and to look forward to the prize of their call in Jesus Christ, because the church had some members who were followers of the circumcision party. The circumcision party is identified as mutilators of the flesh (Phil. 3:2) in the scripture lesson. The aim of the circumcision party was to assert superiority of its Jewish heritage and to compel the gentile Christians to undergo circumcision. This was wrong against the gospel of Jesus Christ, in the opinion of St. Paul. He did not give importance to the religious and social inheritance of Jews, because those prestigious things could create confidence in the flesh or race. St. Paul had inherited those prestigious things, such as, being circumcised on the eighth day, an Israelite, being a Hebrew, being of the tribe of Benjamin, being a law-abiding Pharisee, being religious and blameless (Phil 3:5). He knew that things make one boastful. He reevaluated those prestigious things when he came to know Jesus Christ. He gave up taking pride in those prestigious things of the flesh when he came to know the Lord Jesus Christ. He considered those prestigious things as of no value or worthless when he gained the surpassing greatness of knowing Jesus Christ as his Lord (Phil. 3:7-8). He wanted to be found in Jesus Christ and to have the righteousness of God through the faith in Jesus Christ than his own righteousness based on the law (Phil. 3:9). He knew that he was saved by the grace of God in Jesus Christ. After being saved by grace, he was engaged in preaching the gospel of Jesus Christ. He was waiting to be rewarded for his work for Jesus Christ. He wished other Christians to be like him. Therefore, he wrote to the Christians at Philippi:

> Brethren, I do not consider that I have made it my own but one thing I do, forgetting what lies behind and straining forward to what lies ahead.
> I press on toward the goal for the prize of the upward call of God in Christ Jesus. (Philippians 3:13-14)

This is the text, within its historical setting.

An Analysis of the Text

This text has three ideas. (A) The first idea of the text is that St. Paul told the Philippians that he has not reached his goal as yet.

(B) The second idea is that he does two things-

(i) On one hand, he forgets what lies behind him. (ii) On the other hand, he strains forward to what lies ahead of him.

(C) The third idea is that he presses on toward the goal for the prize of the upward call of God in Jesus Christ.

An Exposition of the Ideas

(A) The first idea of the text is that St. Paul told the Philippians that he has not reached his goal or has not received the prize as yet. We should know what was his ultimate goal. His final objective was to be Christlike in his suffering and resurrection (Phil. 3:10-11). For him, to be Christlike was to be perfect (Phil. 3:12). In another place, he defined the perfection in terms of sharing the glory of the Lord Jesus Christ (II Thes. 2:14).

In order to achieve this spiritual goal, St. Paul was prepared to suffer for the cause of Jesus Christ, which was to spread the gospel of the Lord Jesus Christ. He was ready not to suffer like Jesus Christ but even ready to die like Jesus Christ. He shared in the suffering of Jesus Christ (II Cor. 1:5; 4:10-11; Gal. 6:17). He metaphorically told the church at Colosse that he bore the marks of Jesus Christ on his body (Col. 1:24). In his suffering, he experienced the life of Jesus Christ in his soul. He wrote to the Galatians about this mystical experience, in these words:

> I have been crucified with Christ; it is no longer I who live, but Christ who lives in me. (Gal. 2:20)

This mystical experience, however, was lacking the experience of the power of resurrection and to know subsequently the everlasting life and fellowship with God. He was looking forward to experience these spiritual realities. These would bring him the perfection. In other words, his goal was completely spiritual or heavenwardness. He knew he had to wait for being perfect. He was in the process of becoming perfect. He was sure of attaining his goal and reward after a short time.

(B) The second idea is that he does two things-

(i) On one hand, he forgets what lies behind him. (ii) On the other hand, he strains forward to what lies ahead of him. St. Paul used these techniques to achieve his spiritual goal.

(i) Let us see first the things he had to forget which lay behind him. He had to forget those things which gave every Jew a sense of social and religious pride, enabling them to earn their salvation. He has mentioned those religious and prestigious things in the scripture lesson. We should try to know their importance, from a Jewish point of view.

(a) St. Paul said that he was circumcised on the eighth day. It means that St. Paul was a Jew, practising Judaism from his childhood. It had become a permanent law among the Israel to circumcise a male child on his eighth day. When God made a covenant with Abraham, He commanded:

> This is my covenant, which you shall keep, between me and you and your descendants after you: Every male among you shall be circumcised. You shall be circumcised in the flesh of your foreskins, and it shall be a sign of the covenant between me and you. He that is eight days old among you shall be circumcised; every male throughout your generations, whether born in your house, or bought with your money from any foreigner who is not of your offspring, both he that is born in your house and he that is bought with your money, shall be circumcised. So shall my covenant be in your flesh an everlasting covenant. Any uncircumcised who is not circumcised in the flesh of his foreskin shall be cut off from his people; he has broken my covenant. (Gen. 17:10-14)

This commandment states that circumcision was an external sign of the everlasting covenant between God and Abraham and his descendants. It means that circumcision distinguished Hebrews as the people of God from the gentiles. Hebrews considered themselves as the chosen people of God among the rest of the mankind, because they were circumcised in the flesh. This gave Hebrews a sense of pride.

This commandment states that a male child be circumcised on the eighth day. This commandment was repeated and turned into a permanent law of Hebrews (Lev. 12:3). St. Paul adhered to the commandment when he was a child. This commandment gave a sense of pride to those who were circumcised on the eighth day over those who were circumcised on later days. Ishmaelites were circumcised in their thirteenth year (Gen. 17:25) and the proselytes were circumcised in manhood; they were not circumcised on the eighth day; therefore, they were not genuine Hebrews. St. Paul stressed the fact that he was born into the Jewish faith and he was keeping Jewish ceremonies since his birth. Like other Jews, he also had a reason to put confidence in the flesh. But he gave up this confidence when he came to know Jesus Christ.

(b) St. Paul said that he belonged to the people of Israel. He was Israelite by race. The name 'Israel' was given to Jacob by God after his wresting with an angel of God (Gen. 32:28). The people of Israel traced their heritage to Jacob in a special sense. Ishmaelites could trace their descent to Abraham but not to Jacob directly. Edomintes could trace their descent to Isaac but not to Jacob directly. Only the Israelites could trace their descent to Jacob directly, who God called by name of Israel. By calling himself an Israelite, St. Paul stressed the absolute purity of his race and his descent.[2] Like other Jews, St. Paul had a reason to put his confidence in the flesh; but he gave it up when he came to know Jesus Christ.

(c) St. Paul said that he belonged to the tribe of Benjamin. Benjamin was the child of Rachel, a well-loved wife of Jacob (Gen. 29:18-20, 30). Jacob had twelve sons; eleven of those sons were born outside of the promised land; only Benjamin was born in the promised land (Gen. 35: 16-18). From the tribe of Benjamin, Saul was chosen as the first king of Israel (I Sam. 9:1-2). The original name of St. Paul was Saul. When the kingdom was divided, only the tribe of Benjamin remained faithful with the kings of Judah (I Kg. 12:21). When the Jews were permitted to return to Palestine to build the temple at Jerusalem and to restore the walls of Jerusalem, the exiles from the tribe of Benjamin and from Judah returned and they formed the nucleus of the reborn nation (Ezra 4:1). Because of these reasons, the tribe of Benjamin became an elite of Israel. St. Paul claimed to belong to the elite of Israel. Like other Jews he had a reason to take pride in the flesh, but he gave it up when he came to know Jesus Christ.

(d) St. Paul said that he was a Hebrew of the Hebrews. The Jews were taken into captivity to many cities, such as Rome, Alexandria. Those Jews refused to adopt the religions of other nations; they maintained their own religion, customs, and laws in the foreign lands. Nevertheless, some Jews became Greek-speaking and they forgot their Hebrew tongue. A few Jews made deliberate effort to retain their Hebrew tongue. St. Paul was one of the Jews, retaining Hebrew tongue. He was born in Tarsus, a gentile city, but he went to Jerusalem to be educated in Jewish heritage (Acts 22:3); he spoke to a mob in Jerusalem in Hebrew tongue (Acts 21:40). As he retained Hebrew tongue, he claimed to be a Hebrew of the Hebrews.

(e) St. Paul said that he was a Pharisee with reference to Jewish laws. He was a trained Pharisee (Acts 22:3; 23:6; 26:5). The Pharisees were considered to be the spiritual athletes of Judaism. The name Pharisees means 'The Separated Ones:' who separated themselves from the worldly life in order to keep the Jewish law in its entirety. St. Paul had devoted his life to the most rigorous observance of the Jewish law. Like other Jews he had a reason to be proud of his religious conduct; but he gave the pride when he came to know Jesus Christ.

(ii) The second part of his techniques was to strain himself forward to what lies ahead of him. In other words, St. Paul was concentrating on the goal that was lying before him. He was maintaining his focus on the goal. His concentration on the goal is justifiable with reference to the scripture. Moses told the people of Israel how to keep their goal of entering into the promised land and stay in it, in the following words:

> You shall be careful to do therefore as the LORD your God has commanded you; you shall not turn aside to the right hand or to the left. You shall walk in all the way which the LORD your God has commanded you, that you may live, and that it may go well with you, and that you may live long in the land which you shall possess. (Deut. 5:32-33)

Moses told the people of Israel to concentrate on the command of the LORD God and not to deviate from the path which would lead to their goal. God also gave a similar advice to Joshua in order to be successful in his life, saying:

> Be strong and of good courage; for you shall cause this people to inherit the land which I swore to their fathers to give. Only be strong and very courageous, being careful to do according to all the law which Moses my servant commanded you; turn not from it to the right hand or to the left, that you have good success wherever you go. (Jos. 1:6-7)

The writer of the book of Proverbs similarly wrote:

> Let your eyes look directly forward, and your gaze be straight before you. Take heed to the path of your feet, then all your ways will be sure. Do not swerve to the right or to the left; turn your feet away from evil. (Pr. 4:25-27)

St. Paul followed this scriptural technique in order to achieve what was lying ahead of him, in the next world.

(C) The third idea is that St. Paul presses on toward the goal for the prize of the upward call of God in Jesus Christ. In the previous verse, St. Paul said that he was straining toward what was lying before him. He now went on clarifying his goal in terms of the prize of his upward call of God in Christ Jesus. In the previous verses (Phil 3:10-11), St. Paul stated his goals in this life and beyond this life: to know Jesus Christ, to know the power of his resurrection, to share in the sufferings of Jesus Christ, to become like Jesus Christ in his death, and attain to the resurrection from the dead. These goals constitute "the surpassing greatness of knowing Jesus Christ my Lord" (Phil.3:8). With reference to this surpassing greatness, St. Paul gave up his racial and religious claims and thought of those claims as rubbish.

Let us reflect on the goal of the life of St. Paul. His goal in this human life was to share in the sufferings of Jesus Christ and even to become like Jesus Christ in his death. He considered this as his privilege to share in the sufferings of Jesus Christ. He mentioned those sufferings for Jesus Christ, in the following passage:

> Five times I have received at the hands of the Jews forty lashes less one. Three times I have been beaten with rods; once I was stoned. Three times I have been shipwrecked; a night and a day I have been adrift at sea; on frequent journeys, in danger from rivers, dangers from robbers, danger from my own people, danger from Gentiles, danger in the city, danger in the wilderness, danger at sea, danger from false brethren; in toil and hardship, through many a sleepless night, in hunger and thirst, in cold and exposure. And apart from these things, there is the daily pressure upon me of my anxiety for all the churches. (II Cor. 11:24-28)

St. Paul suffered these things for the sake of Jesus Christ, his Lord. He was even ready to die like Jesus Christ, on the cross. After persecutions and tortures, St. Paul was beheaded by the Roman Emperor Nero (A. D. 54-68) at Rome.

St. Paul's other goals are mystical and to be fulfilled beyond the grave. He began to experience the mystical presence of Jesus Christ in his life. He wrote to the believers at Galatia:

> I have been crucified with Christ; it is no longer I who live, but Christ who lives in me. (Gal. 2:20)

However, he was not content with this experience. He wished to experience the power of the resurrection of Jesus Christ and to have everlasting fellowship with Him and to have the everlasting life. This was the perfection he ultimately aimed at. This was the most intimate mystical and personal knowledge of God. St. Paul wanted to have this knowledge. This goal was other worldly and to be fulfilled beyond the grave.

Conclusion

St. Paul's final goal was to have the most intimate mystical knowledge of God in Jesus Christ. In order to achieve this goal, he gave up his prestigious claims and accepted to suffer like Jesus Christ. He concentrated on his spiritual goal; he did not turn either to the right or to the left. This was his way of running his spiritual race. All believers should aspire towards this goal and practise what St. Paul did.

Recommended Hymns from the Methodist Hymnal

492 'I the good fight have fought,'

553 'Come, Holy Ghost, all-quickening fire!'

579 'Saviour, Thy dying love'

672 'Saviour blessed Saviour,'

Endnotes

[1] *The New American Encyclopedia*, (Philadelphia /Munich: The Publishers Agency Inc., 1974), Vol. 15, p.5394

[2] William Barclay, *The Letters to Philippians Colossians Thessalonians*, (Edinburgh: The Saint Andrew Press, Third Impression, 1963), p. 72.

Chapter 14

'Purified Vessel of the Lord,' 'Consecrated and Useful Vessels of the Master,' 'Noble Use Demanding Consecration,' 'Spiritual Preparation for the Lord's Work,' 'Spiritual Fitness.'

Scripture

II Timothy 2:14-26

Numbers 16:1-35

Isaiah 52:11

II Corinthians 6:14 -7:1

Ephesians 4:11-12; 5:8-11

Text: II Timothy 2:21

A Few Versions of the Text, II Timothy 2:21

Therefore if anyone cleanses himself from the latter, he will be a vessel for honor, sanctified and useful for the Master, prepared for every good work. *New King James Version*

If a man therefore purge himself from these, he shall be a vessel unto honour, consecrated, and fit for the Master's use, prepared for every good work. *Explanatory Notes Upon the New Testament*

If any one purifies himself from what is ignoble, then he will be a vessel for noble use, consecrated and useful to the master of the house, ready for any good work. *Revised Standard Version*

If a man cleanses himself from the latter, he will be an instrument for noble purposes, made holy, useful to the Master, prepared to do any good work. *New International Version*

To be among those which are valued dedicated, a thing of use to the Master of the house, a man must cleanse himself from all those evil things; then he will be fit for any honourable purpose. *The New English Bible*

If you stay away from sin you will be like one of these dishes made of purest gold- the very best in the house- so that Christ himself can use you for his highest purposes. *The Living Bible Illustrated*

Those who stop associating with dishonorable people will be honored. They will be set apart for the master's use, prepared to do good things. *God's Word*

Introduction

(1) Persons who wish to participate in Olympic games have to make their bodies fit for the games. They have to take exercises daily and eat nutritious food. They have to avoid certain things and do certain things to make their bodies fit. If their bodies are not well or unfit for any reason, they would not be able to participate in competitions.

(2) There are requirements of fitness in other areas of life. There was a young musician in the royal band of Hanover. Because of his remarkable skill, he was promoted to march at the head of the troops, discoursing martial music. He went to a war. He had to lie in the trenches all night. He was not able to stand that discomfort. One night he deserted the army and fled to England. It was a serious crime for a soldier to desert an army. The penalty for desertion was death. He was not caught and punished for the crime.

He became a great organist. His interest was also in astronomy. With great pains he constructed a telescope and discovered a new planet called Uranus in 1871. For this discovery the Royal Society awarded him with a Copley medal. He was able to observe the seventh satellite in the Saturn system in 1789 for the first time.[1] He received the applause of the whole world. His name was Frederick William Herschel (1738-1822).

He was sent for by the king; he went to Windsor Castle. The king's name was George II of Hanover (1683-1760) the sovereign to whom his life was a forfeit for his old desertion. King George II of Hanover knew him to be a deserter.

Before the king could see him, he was asked to open an envelop containing a royal communication. He did so, wondering what the king was going to do with him. The royal communication was the royal pardon to him. By the royal pardon, the deserter was made fit to meet the king. King George II said to him, "Now, we can talk, and you shall come up and live at Windsor and be Sir William Herschel."[2]

(3) There was a soldier in the army of Alexander the Great (356-323 B. C.). He was brought before the great world-conqueror for martial court. When the emperor had listened to the charges and saw the evidences, the emperor turned to the soldier facing condemnation, and asked the guilty soldier his name, "What is your name?" The soldier replied, "Alexander." Again the emperor asked, "What is your name?" The second time the soldier answered, "Alexander!" With a rage, the emperor roared, "I say, what is your name?" The soldier gave the reply, "Alexander!" Alexander the Great angrily said to the soldier, "You say your name is Alexander? You are found guilty of your crime as charged, and now you must pay the penalty. Either change your conduct or change your name, for no man can bear the name of Alexander, my name, and do the things that you have done."[3] This event tells us that conduct of a person must fit his or her name.

Introduction of the Text

The principle of fitness applies to a spiritual life and profession of Christians. When believers are addressed as Christians or the followers of Jesus Christ, they have to show their Christlike characteristics to others. They have to be worthy vessels of Jesus Christ. St. Paul exhorted Christians in the following words:

> **If any one purifies himself from what is ignoble, then he will be a vessel for noble use, consecrated and useful to the master of the house, ready for any good work. (II Tim. 2:21)**

This is the text of our meditation now.

The Context of the Text

Apostle Paul was talking about a good leadership as opposed to bad leadership in a church. He mentioned two leaders, namely, Hymenaeus and Philetus. Those two leaders were teaching about Christian faith in the resurrection of human bodies. But their teaching about the physical resurrection was not in harmony with the teaching of Jesus Christ about resurrection. Hymenaeus and Philetus taught that the resurrection of body had already happened, either at the moment of baptism or in man's children. This kind of teaching undermined the central and essential belief of the Christian faith. With reference to those leaders, St. Paul said, "The Lord knows those who are his;" and "let every one who names the name of the Lord depart from iniquity." (II Tim. 2:19). Those two leaders had an evil influence on other Christians, who were following them. St. Paul explained their presence in the church of God in terms of vessels for ignoble use. Those leaders were used for stupid and senseless controversies; they were quarrelsome and impolite. St. Paul exhorted other Christian leaders, saying:

> If any one purifies himself from what is ignoble, then he will be a vessel for noble use, consecrated and useful to the master of the house, ready for any good work. (II Tim. 2:21)

This is the text, within its historical setting.

An Analysis of the Text

This text contains two ideas. (A) The first idea is a conditional statement saying, "If any one purifies himself from what is ignoble."

(B) The second idea is the result of the purification. The person will be a vessel for noble use; he will be consecrated and useful to the master of the house, ready for any good work.

An Exposition of the Ideas

(A) The first idea of the text is a conditional statement saying, "If any one purifies himself from what is ignoble." Apostle Paul said this to Christians and their leaders. This means that he said this to the people who were already in a church. Before those Christians and their leaders embraced Christian faith, they heard the gospel of Jesus Christ through the apostles of Jesus Christ. They learned about forgiveness of sin through their faith in the blood of Jesus Christ. Before they became Christians, they were told by the apostles of Christ that they were away from the living God and they needed to go to God for salvation. They were told what was noble and right in the sight of God, and what was ignoble and wrong in His sight. Having learned about these spiritual matters, they received the baptism and became members of churches (cf. Eph. 5:8-11). Being a member of a church is an obligation of holiness of heart and life. God's people would be separated from the other people in the world. There are a few events to illustrate the point.

(1) When Korah, Dathan, and Abiram rebelled against leadership and authority of Moses and priestly privilege of Aaron (Num. 16:1-3), it displeased the LORD God (Num. 16:20) and His servant Moses (Num. 16:15-17). When those rebellious leaders refused to go to the tabernacle, Moses took the elders of Israel with him and went to the tents of Korah, Dathan, and Abiram. Moses then said to the congregation:

> Depart, I pray you, from the tents of these wicked men, and touch nothing of theirs, lest you be swept away with all their sins. (Num. 16:26)

Moses then asked God to open earth's mouth; and let the followers of Korah, Dathan, and Abiram be swallowed up, because they despised the LORD. After this address, the mouth of the earth was opened; and swallowed the wicked leaders and their followers (Num. 16:30-33). This event confirmed who were the consecrated servants of the LORD God; and demonstrated how the defiant wicked servants of God were punished for their sin.

(2) The LORD God, who is pure and holy, wants His people to be pure and consecrated. The LORD God sent to the people of Judah, in their captivity, the message through prophet Isaiah as follows:

> Depart, depart, go out thence, touch no unclean thing; go out from the midst of her, purify yourselves, you who bear the vessels of the LORD. (Is. 52:11)

What was expected of old Israel was similarly expected of the Church, the new Israel. Apostle Paul wrote to Christians at Corinth as to why they have to separate from the world in order to be God's people, as follows:

> Do not be mismated with unbelievers. For what partnership have righteousness with iniquity? Or what fellowship has light with darkness? What accord has Christ with Belial? Or what has a believer in common with an unbeliever? What agreement has the temple of God with idols? For we are the temple of the living God; as God said, 'I will live in them and move among them, and I will be their God, and they shall be my people. Therefore come out from them, and be separate from them, says the LORD, and touch nothing unclean; then I will welcome you, and you shall be my sons and daughters, says the LORD Almighty.' Since we have these promises, beloved, let us cleanse ourselves from every defilement of body and spirit, and make holiness perfect in the fear of God. (II Cor. 6:14 -7:1)

As Christians are chosen people of God, they have to keep away from doing ignoble or wicked things. They cannot be true Christians while they continue to do ignoble things. The word of God tells them to purify themselves from the ignoble things.

(B) The second idea of the text is the result of the purification. The person will be a vessel for noble use; he will be consecrated and useful to the master of the house, ready for any good work. One of the noble uses of the purified servants of the Lord Jesus is that they preach and teach the gospel of the Lord Jesus with honesty and integrity. There are always temptations to preach and teach whatever pleases the people, even at the cost of the doctrines of Christian faith. The teachers and preachers dilute the doctrines of Christian faith to suit to the taste of the audience. Such presentation would be full of lies; and it would deceive many believers. This problem occurred in the early church. Therefore, St. Paul wrote to Titus against the empty talkers and deceivers the following words:

> But as for you, teach what befits sound doctrine. Bid the older men be temperate, serious, sensible, sound in faith, in love, and in steadfastness. Bid the older women likewise to be reverent in behaviour, not to be slanderers or slaves to drink; they are to teach what is good, and so train the young women to love their husbands and children, to be sensible, chaste, domestic, kind, submissive to their husbands, that the word of God may not be discredited. Likewise urge the younger men to control themselves. Show yourself in all respects a model of good deeds, and in your teaching show integrity, gravity, and sound speech that cannot be censured, so that an opponent may be put to shame, having nothing evil to say of us. (Tit. 2:1-8)

The preachers and teachers of the gospel of Lord Jesus Christ have to impart the word of God with integrity; they have to practise what they teach or preach.

Apart from teaching and preaching the word of God, there are some other social and charitable services to be rendered by the Church (Eph. 4:11-12). Those services should be rendered by the consecrated servants of the Lord Jesus Christ. Those servants should be ready for any work. Those services may be humble, others may bring honour and prestige to the servants.

In Christian ministry, primary emphasis is not upon personal capacity or worth of servants; but it is upon the spiritual fitness of the servants. An emphasis is not upon hard and demanding service. Hard and demanding services may bring honour and glory to the servants;

they may be honoured for their exceptional services. However, servants of the Lord Jesus Christ should not think of glory and honour, but they should think of making them fit for the service of the Lord Jesus Christ.

Conclusion

Every servant of Jesus Christ, who is willing to render whatever service is required in the name of Jesus Christ, must be first cleansed from all kinds of spiritual defilement. Then they will be fitting vessels for any noble purpose of the Lord Jesus Christ. The spiritual fitness of the savants is more important than the prestige and honour which the services carry with them.

Recommended Hymns for the Methodist Hymnal
9 'O Worship the Lord in the'

36 'Holy, holy, holy, Lord God Almighty!'

37 'Hail! holy, holy, holy Lord!'

394 'Just as I am, Thine own to be,'

400 'Take my life, and let it be'

744 'O Happy day that fixed my choice'

Recommended Responsive Reading from the Methodist Hymnal
35 (p. 398),

Recommended Responsive Reading from A Worship Manual for Scriptural or Methodist Order of Service
28 (pp. 115-116).

Endnotes
[1] *The New American Encyclopedia*, Vol.10, p.3363.

[2] Paul Lee Tan, *Encyclopedia of 7700 Illustration: Signs of the Times*, # 5370.

[3] Paul Lee Tan, op.cit., # 4999.

Chapter 15

'Negative and Positive Sides of God's Grace,' 'Training of God's Grace,' 'Renunciation of Irreligion and Affirmation of Religion,' 'Balancing Negative and Positive Sides of God's Grace'

Scripture

Titus 2:1-14

Genesis 15:1-6

II Kings 9:6-10, 22-26, 30-37; 10:6-11, 18-27, 31; 22:3-7, 14-17; 23:1-7, 10, 12-13, 15, 19-25

Psalms 32:1-2; 119:89

Isaiah 29:14; 40:8; 57:10

Jeremiah 4:22

Matthew 24:25

Romans 1:22; 4:4-12; 5:1-2, 15-17

I Corinthians 3:19

Ephesians 2:7-8

Galatians 3:6-9

II Timothy 3:16-17

Titus 1:2, 7-9

James 3:15

I Peter 1:25

II Peter 1:16

Text: Titus 2:11-12

A Few Versions of the Text, Titus 2:11-12

For the grace of God that brings salvation has appeared to all men, teaching us that denying ungodliness and worldly lusts, we should live and soberly, righteously, and godly in the present world, *The New King James Version*

For the saving grace of God hath appeared to all men, instructing us that, having renounced ungodliness and all worldly desires, we should live soberly, and righteously, and godly in the present world; *Explanatory Notes Upon the New Testament*

For the grace of God has appeared for the salvation of all men, training us to renounce irreligion and worldly passions, and to lead sober, upright, and godly lives in this world, *Revised Standard Version*

For the grace of God that brings salvation has appeared to all men. It teaches us to say "No" to ungodliness and worldly passions, and to live self-controlled, upright and godly lives in this present age, *New International Version*

For the grace of God has dawned upon the world with healing for all mankind; and by it we are disciplined to renounce godless ways and worldly desires, and to live a life of temperance, honesty, sober, and godliness in the present age, *The New English Bible*

For the free gift of eternal salvation is now being offered to everyone; and along with this gift comes the realization that God wants us to turn from godless living and sinful pleasures and to live good, God-fearing lives day after day, *The Living Bible Illustrated*

After all, God's saving kindness has appeared for the benefit of all people. It trains us to avoid ungodly lives filled with worldly desires, so that we can live self-controlled, moral, and godly lives in this present world. *God's Word*

Introduction

It would be always appropriate to bear testimony about how the holy scriptures or the Bible influenced the life of the believers. God is the final source of the word of God, the Bible. His servants were filled with the Holy Spirit to speak and to write the word of God (II Pet. 1:16). As God is the source of the holy scriptures, the truth of the word of God stands for ever (Ps. 119:89; Is. 40:8; Mt. 24:25; I Pet. 1:25). The Bible had been the teacher of mankind from generation to generation. It has changed many lives positively; it has left a permanent impression on the lives of many people. The work of the word of God is stated in these words:

> All scripture is inspired by God and profitable for teaching, for reproof, for correction, and for training in righteousness, that the man of God may be complete, equipped for every good work. (II Tim. 3:16-17)

The word of God is the teacher for all- poor and rich, illiterate and educated, simple minded and very wise. It teaches man, irrespective of his or her status in life.

John Selden (1584-1654) was a wealthy and highly learned man. He had 8,000 volumes in his personal library. As he was about to die, Archbishop James Usher (January 4,1581-March 21, 1656) went to see him. In their last conversation, John Selden said to Archbishop James Usher:

> I have surveyed most of the learning that is among the sons of men, and my study is filled with books and manuscripts on various subjects. But

at present I cannot recollect any passage out of all my books and papers whereon I can rest my soul, save this from the sacred Scripture. 'The grace of God that bringeth salvation hath appeared to all men, teaching us that, denying ungodliness and worldly lusts, we should live soberly, righteously, and godly, in this present world; looking for that blessed hope, and the glorious appearing of the great God and our Saviour Jesus Christ; who gave Himself for us, that He might redeem us from all iniquity, and purify unto Himself- a peculiar people, zealous for good works.'[1]

In these words, John Selden, a distinguished scholar in wisdom, gave the testimony about the holy scriptures that it left a permanent impression on his mind, at the point of his death. It means that the understanding and wisdom, which come from the holy scriptures, supersedes the worldly knowledge. The worldly knowledge is not everlasting (Is. 29:14; 57:10). It is foolishness in the sight of God (Rom. 1:22; I Cor. 3:19). It is earthly, unspiritual, and devilish (Jas. 3:15). It cannot satisfy man's spiritual thirst and hunger.

The understanding and wisdom that comes from the word of God is spiritual and divine. The people of God must study the holy scriptures for enlightenment. If they neglect the study of the word of God, they would be foolish and wicked. God said so through prophet Jeremiah:

> For my people are foolish, they know me not; they are stupid children, they have no understanding. They are skilled in doing evil, but how to do good they know not. (Jer. 4:22)

As long as churchgoers are not ready to learn more and more from the word of God, they will not be able to do what is right and just. They will be proud of their foolish ways and wicked actions, until they know the word of God properly and thoroughly. John Selden learned to know a true source of knowledge which is the sacred scripture. We should believe in his honest testimony.

Introduction of the Text

John Selden, who studied all the books, which were available in the world of his time, bore the witness that he could not remember any passage from other books except from the holy scripture [Titus 2:11-14], exhorting mankind to give up wickedness and walk in righteousness; these are the two aspects of the grace of God. Out of this passage we shall select two verses, for our mediation, as follow:

> **For the grace of God has appeared for the salvation of all men, training us to renounce irreligion and worldly passions, and to lead sober, upright, and godly lives in this world,** (Titus 2:11-12).

The Context of the Text

St. Paul wrote this letter to Titus. Titus was appointed as the bishop of churches in Crete (Tit. 1:2) by St. Paul. St. Paul exhorted Titus about the character and duties of a bishop (Tit. 1:7-9). The main duty of the bishop is to teach sound doctrines of Christian faith. The practical aspect of this duty is to exhort the older men and older women to set their good examples before younger men and women (Tit. 2:2-3). The young men and slaves [servants] were exhorted to be obedient to their elderly persons and to the masters (Tit. 2:6-10). St. Paul believed that Christians were chosen by Jesus Christ; therefore, they should be zealous for good deeds (Tit.2:14). God in Jesus Christ chose Christians as His people for holiness and righteousness. In other words, the saving grace of God has effect on the character of man. The saving grace of God in Jesus Christ has two sides- negative and positive- which call the believers to renounce wickedness and embrace righteousness. This idea is stated in these words:

> For the grace of God has appeared for the salvation of all men, training us to renounce irreligion and worldly passions, and to lead sober, upright, and godly lives in this world,.... (Tit. 2:11-12)

This is the text, within its historical setting.

An Analysis of the Text

This text has two ideas. (A) The first idea is that the grace of God is given to all people.

(B) The second idea is that the grace of God has two sides. The first side of the grace is negative, in terms of renouncing irreligion and worldly passions. The second side is positive, in terms of leading sober, upright, and godly lives in this world.

An Exposition of the Textual Ideas

(A) The first idea of the text is that the grace of God is given to all people. It means salvation of all people by the grace of God, and not by good deeds of man. The Jews and Gentiles were to be saved by the grace of God. This universal way of salvation was proclaimed by the word of God. But this doctrine was not clearly stated until St. Paul began to preach the gospel, the good news of salvation to the Jews and the Gentiles. When Abram was without a son from Sarah, God promised him to give him a son and multiply his descendants numerously. Abram believed the promise of God and his belief was reckoned to him as righteousness (Gen. 15:1-6).

St. Paul developed the idea of salvation of all by the faith in God. He wrote to the Galatians:

> Thus Abraham believed God, and it was reckoned to him as righteousness.' So you see that it is men of faith who are the sons of Abraham. And the scripture, foreseeing that God would justify the Gentiles by faith, preached the gospel beforehand to Abraham, saying, 'In you shall all the nations be blessed.' So then, those who are men of faith are blessed with Abraham who had faith. (Gal. 3:6-9)

This idea is elaborated by St. Paul in his letter to the Romans:

> For if Abraham was justified by works, he has something to boast about, but not before God. For what does the scripture say? 'Abraham believed God, and it was reckoned to him a righteousness.' [Gen. 16:6] Now to one who works, his wages are not reckoned as a gift but his due. And to one who does not work but trust him who justifies the ungodly, his faith is reckoned as righteousness. So also David pronounces a blessing upon the man to whom God reckons righteousness apart from work:

> 'Blessed are those whose iniquities are forgiven, and whose sins are covered; blessed is the man against whom the Lord will not reckon his sin.' [Ps. 32:1-2]

> Is this blessing pronounced only upon the circumcised, or also upon the uncircumcised? We say that faith was reckoned to Abraham as righteousness. How then was it reckoned to him? Was it before or after he had been circumcised? It was not after, but before he was circumcised. He received circumcision as a sign or seal of the righteousness which he had by faith while he was uncircumcised. The purpose was to make him

the father of all who believe without being circumcised and who thus have righteousness reckoned to them, and likewise the father of the circumcised who are not merely circumcised but who follow the example of faith which our father Abraham had before he was circumcised. (Rom. 4:2-12)

St. Paul preached this doctrine of salvation by the grace of God in Jesus Christ to all the people (Rom. 5:1-2, 15-17; Eph. 2:7-8).

(B) The second idea of the text is that the grace of God has two sides. The first side of the grace is negative, in terms of renouncing irreligion and worldly passions. The second side is positive, in terms of leading sober, upright, and godly lives in this world. Let us deal with these two sides of the grace of God in the life of the believers.

(1) The first side of the grace is negative, in terms of (a) renouncing irreligion and (b) renouncing worldly passions.

(a) Renouncing irreligion means giving up bad religion or wrong religion. Bad religion is against the true religion; the true religion is righteousness and piety in the sight of the LORD God. The word of God commands the worshippers to worship God only, and not to serve and bow down before false gods. The people of Israel and of Judah were not keeping the command of God to serve and worship Him only. Some of them were worshipping foreign gods. Even some of the kings of those two kingdoms patronized the worship of foreign gods. King Ahab (869-850 B. C.) and his wife Jezebel patronized the worship of Baal. God was displeased with king Ahab; He decided to remove King Ahab from the throne, and to give his throne to his servant.

The LORD God asked prophet Elisha to anoint Jehu to be the successor of King Ahab and to ask Jehu (842-815 B. C.) to execute the following commissions:

Thus says the LORD the God of Israel, I anoint you king over the people of the LORD, over Israel. And you shall strike down the house of Ahab your master, that I may avenge of Jezebel the blood of my servants the prophets, the blood of all the servants of the LORD. For the whole house of Ahab shall perish; and I will cut off from Ahab every male, bond and free, in Israel. And I will make the house of Ahab like the house of

> Jeroboam the son of Nabat, and like the house Baasha the son of Ahijah.
> And the dogs shall eat Jezebel in the territory of Jezreel, and none shall
> bury her. (II Kg. 9:6-10)

Jehu was proclaimed to be the king of Israel by other commanders of Ahab. Jehu went from Ramoth-gilead to Jezreel, where Joram, a son of King Ahab, was living. Joram went to see Jehu at the property of Naboth. Jehu killed Joram there. (II Kg. 9:22-26) Then Jehu went to Jezereel. He went to the palace where Queen Jezebel was residing. Jehu asked three eunuchs, the guards, to throw Queen Jezebel down from her palace. They threw her down and she was killed. Her body was eaten by dogs. (II Kg. 9:30-37) Then Jehu ordered killing of seventy sons, and all relatives of King Ahab, living in Samaria. (II Kg. 10:6-11) Then he killed all priests of Baal and destroyed the temple of Baal. (II Kg. 10:18-27)

King Jehu (842-815 B. C.) was instrumental to carry out the negative side of a religious reform in the life of the kingdom of Israel. God established the throne of King Jehu until his fourth generation. But King Jehu himself was not careful to walk in the law of the LORD God with all his heart (II Kg. 10:31). He failed to carry out the positive side of the religious reform in his private and social life.

(b) Renouncing irreligion goes with renouncing worldly passions, because they go together. The Baal worship was immoral religion, because it was a form of a fertility cult. There was a practice of male cult prostitution in the temple of Asherah (II Kg. 23:7). These worldly passions are identified as fornication and impurity. St. Paul added other evil passions as worldly passions, such as evil desire, covetousness, anger, wrath, malice, slander, foul talk, and lying (Col.3, 5, 8-9). Satisfaction or fulfilment of these worldly passions leads man to sin and makes him an enemy of God, therefore, His wrath kindles against sins of man. St. James, in his exhortation to Christians said the following words:

> Unfaithful creatures! Do you not know that the friendship with the world
> is enmity with God? Therefore whoever wishes to be a friend of the world
> makes himself an enemy of God. (Jas. 4:5)

God does not approve the satisfaction of the worldly passions, because He is the righteous, pure, and holy God. He commands His people to be holy and just as He is holy and righteous. Therefore, God's chosen people have to renounce irreligion and worldly passions.

(2) The second side of the grace of God is positive, in terms of leading sober, upright, and godly lives in this world. The holy and righteous God would be pleased with the persons, who renounce irreligion and worldly passions, which is the negative side of the grace of God, operating in the life of the persons. But the same God would be more pleased with those, who enforce the positive side of the grace of God in their life.

King Josiah (640-609 B. C.), from his childhood, began to do what was right in the sight of God; and he followed the way of David. He remained faithful to God. When he was twenty-six years old, he sent Shaphan, the secretary, to Hilkiah, the high priest, to use the money of the people toward repairs of the temple. (II Kg. 22:3-7). While the repairs to the temple were carried on, somebody found the book of the law in the temple. Hilkiah gave the book to Shaphan. Shaphan read the book to King Josiah. When the king heard the book of the law, he rent his clothes. He commanded Hilkiah, Shaphan, and Asiah, a servant of the king, to inquire of the LORD's judgment and wrath on him and his people. They went to see Huldah, the prophetess, who confirmed God's wrath against the people in Judah (II Kg. 22:14-17).

King Josiah commanded all the elders of Judah and Jerusalem to gather in the temple. He read the law of God to them; and he made a covenant before the LORD to walk after the LORD and to keep His commandments. All the people followed the king in renewing their covenant with God (II Kg. 23:1-3).

As a result of renewing the covenant with God to serve Him and obey His commandment, King Josiah ordered Hilkiah, other priests, and keepers of the temple to bring out the vessels made for Baal, for Asherah, and for other gods, from the temple. He burned those vessels in the fields of Kidron. He carried their ashes to Bethel, where the people of the kingdom of Israel were worshipping other gods (II Kg. 23:4-5). The king removed the priests, from Jerusalem and Judah, who were burning incense to other gods (II Kg. 23:5). He burned the Asherah and reduced them to dust (II Kg. 23:6). He broke down the houses of the male cult prostitutes (II Kg. 23:7). He defiled all the high places in Judah and defiled Topheth, where children were sacrificed to Molech (II Kg. 23:10). He defiled all altars built by other kings for other gods, in Jerusalem (II Kg. 23:12-13).

King Josiah carried the reform movement to the kingdom of Israel and destroyed the altar at Bethel and turned into dust; he burned the Asherah (II Kg. 23:15). He destroyed all the shrines in Samaria (II Kg. 23:19). He also killed the priests of other gods. Then he returned to Jerusalem (II Kg. 23:20).

Having done the negative side of the religious reform, King Josiah turned to the positive side of the reform. In the same year of his eighteenth year of reign, i. e, 622 B. C., he commanded the people of Judah and Israel to keep the Passover feast to the LORD God. That Passover feast was so great or impressive that such was not kept by any king of Judah and Israel (II Kg.23:22). He sincerely attempted to establish the law of the LORD God in Jerusalem and Judah (II Kg. 23:24). He was an ideal king. The writer of the Book of II Kings wrote the praiseworthy words of King Josiah, as follows:

> Before him there was no king like him, who turned to the LORD with all his heart and with all his soul and with all his might, according to the law of Moses; nor did any like him arise after him. (II Kg. 23:25)

The positive side of the grace of God in the life of the believers is that they should be sober, upright, and godly in this world (Tit. 2:14); and they should be zealous for good deeds (Tit. 2:14). This is a general statement about how Christians should act positively. There are specific stipulations for all Christians, in the scripture lesson. The older men should be temperate, serious, sensible, sound in faith, in love and in steadfastness (Tit. 2:2). The older women should train the young women to love their husbands and children, to be sensible, chaste, domestic, kind, and submissive to their husbands, that the word of God may not be discredited (Tit.2:3-5). Young men should control themselves, show themselves in all respects a model of good deeds, and in their teaching they should show integrity and gravity; and they should have sound speech (Tit. 2:7-8).

Both sides of the grace of God in the life of people are equally important. Renouncing irreligion and affirming religion need to be balanced. Jesus Christ made this point in his parable, which can be known as 'the parable of the cleaned and empty house.' Jesus told the parable as follows:

> When the unclean spirit has gone out of a man, he passes through waterless place seeking rest. Finding none he says, 'I will return to my house from which I came.' And when he comes he finds it swept and put in order. Then he goes and brings seven other spirits more evil than himself, and they enter and dwell there; and the last state of that man becomes worse than the first. (Lk. 11:24-26)

In other words, making heart empty of evil passions for time being is not good enough; it has to be filled with good resolve and good deeds. Otherwise, the spiritual condition of man becomes worse than before. A positive side of the grace of God is more important than the negative side of it.

Conclusion

Whenever we think of reforming or reviving the life of the believers or a congregation, we should first think of the ways of removing wickedness, or we should first think of the negative side of the grace of God in the life of the believers. We should prepare the good ground before sowing good seeds. Otherwise, there would be weeds and no crop in the field. Having helped the people to remove the evil passions from their hearts, preachers should sow the seeds of positive desires in the hearts of the people. This was the intent of St. Paul when he wrote to Titus, the words of the text, as follows:

For the grace of God has appeared for the salvation of all men, training us to renounce irreligion and worldly passions, and to lead sober, upright, and godly lives in this world, (Tit. 2:11-12)

Recommended Hymns from the Methodist Hymnal

390 'Give me the faith which can remove'

452 'What shall I do my God to love,'

576 'Be it my only wisdom here'

578 'A charge to keep I have,'

582 'Brightly beams our Father's mercy'

589 'Go, labour on; spend, and be spent,'

594 'Lord, in the strength of grace,'

Endnote

[1] Paul Lee Tan, *Encyclopedia of 7700 Illustrations: Signs of the Time*, #2097

Part II

'METHODIST PIETY AND SOCIAL MORALITY OR SCRIPTURAL HOLINESS OF METHODISM'

"Methodist Piety and
Social Morality"
or
"Scriptural Holiness
of Methodism"

The title of this short essay, "Methodist Piety and Social Morality" or "Scriptural Holiness of Methodism" suggests the scope of the essay in terms of confining our research to the questions as follow: What is a historical background of Methodist piety or holiness? How did the founders of Methodism enforce the principles of social morality? And how did they define the concept of piety or holiness?

A Historical Background of Methodist Piety or Holiness

The Reverend John Wesley (June 17, 1703-March 2, 1791) and the Reverend Charles Wesley (December 18,1707-March 29,1788) were the founders of Methodism. They founded the first Methodist Society at Foundry in London in 1739. Thirty years after the date of organized Methodism, John Wesley wrote to his brother Charles Wesley concerning their ancestry:

> So far as I can learn, such a thing has scarce been for these thousand years before, as a son, father, grandfather, *atavus, tritavus*, preaching the Gospel, nay, the genuine Gospel, in a line.[1]

John Wesley could have equally said that his female ancestors his mother, grandmother, and great- grandmother were distinguished women. Their both male and female ancestors upheld the principles of intellectual, social, and religious nobility and thus contributed toward development and maturity of evangelical conviction in John and Charles Wesley.

The Reverend Bartholomew Wesley (1595 -1680) was the great grandfather of John Wesley. He was a Puritan clergyman in the established church. In 1640 he was appointed the rector of Charmouth. After the Restoration or the Act of Uniformity of 1660, Charles Stuart ejected all the Puritan rectors, therefore the Rev. Bartolomew Wesley lost his parish in 1662.[2] Nevertheless, he continued to preach as a Nonconformist pastor of a portion of his old parishioners till his death in 1680.

The Reverend John Wesley (1636-1678) was the son of the Rev. Bartholomew Wesley and the grandfather of John Wesley. He was consecrated to the ministry in his infancy. He studied at Oxford University. After graduation he began preaching as minister of a congregation at Whitchurch. He defended his right as a Nonconformist. He was imprisoned in 1661 for not using the Book of Common Prayer. He suffered much during the persecution times of the Restoration. He married a daughter of Rev. John White who was a Puritan. He faced religious persecution for a long time. He died at Preston in 1678 at age fortytwo.

Samuel Wesley (April 23,1662-April 25, 1735) was a son of the Rev. John Wesley (1636-1678), born at Whitchurch in 1662. When he was about twenty years old, he was asked to answer some bitter criticisms against the Dissenters or Nonconformists, he studied the subject and decided to leave the Nonconformity and go over to the Church of England. He joined the Oxford University, entering Exeter College in 1682.[3] He left the Nonconformist group and joined the Established church at age twenty. His character ripened at Oxford. He began to show a true pastoral feeling of compassion and responsibility by visiting the prisoners in the castle. He received his B. A. in 1688, signing his name Wesley instead of Westley. He was ordained a deacon and a priest. He was appointed a naval chaplain. He married Susanna Annesley, a daughter of the Rev. Dr. Samuel Annesley, a Puritan, in 1689. He became a rector at Epworth. They had nineteen children in twentyone years. John (June 17, 1703-March 2, 1791) was the fifteenth and Charles (December 18,1707-March 29,1788), the eighteenth of the nineteen children, born at Epworth.

This is a brief history of the ancestry of John and Charles Wesley, as far as their male ancestors are concerned. After this, we should know a brief history of their ancestry as far as their female ancestors are concerned.

Susanna Wesley (January 20, 1669-July 23,1742) was the mother of John and Charles Wesley. She was a daughter of the Rev. Dr. Samuel Annesley (1620 December 31, -1696) who was called 'St. Paul of the Nonconformists'.[4] His second wife was a daughter of John White, a man of a highest repute and a Puritan; she was a woman of remarkable piety and she was the mother of Susanna Wesley.[5]

Susanna Annesley was interested in the ecclesiastical and doctrinal controversies of her days, at age thirteen. She was independent in thinking; she expressed her opinions against the church of her father and renounced the Nonconformists and entered the Established Church, one year after Samuel Wesley had come to the same decision. Samuel Wesley met her and they got married in 1689.[6]

Samuel and Susanna Wesley both had a pietistic background. They raised their children, John and Charles and other children in Christian piety, when she went back to the Church of England. Buoy commented on this event when he wrote:

> The Puritan movement in which she had been reared went with her into the Church of England. She entered it essentially a Puritan, and that stern, heroic faith, softened by the grace of God, held her all her life. There was a providence leading this woman back to Anglicanism as plain as that which led the mother of Moses back to the court of Egypt, and she, like Jochebed, had her ministry to train a child who should set the people free.[7]

Susanna also directed her children in the movement of Methodism. Therefore, she was considered to be the mother of Methodism. Isaac Taylor (A. D. 1787-1865) said:

> The Wesley's mother was the mother of Methodism in a religious and moral sense; for her courage, her submissiveness to authority, the high tone of her mind, its independence and its selfcontrol, the warmth of her devotional feelings, and the practical direction given to them, came up, and were visibly repeated in the character and conduct of her sons.[8]

She lived to see England awakening at the call of her sons and she rejoiced to see the multitudes quickened by the new life and new fellowship among Christians.[9]

As the Wesley children owed to their mother, Susanna Wesley, they also owed to their father Samuel Wesley. He was a learned man, a comprehensive thinker, a writer, a speaker, and a hard worker. He was loving, liberal, and true. He was their friend and teacher. He taught them the rudiments of classics. He made them to love reading.[10]

The Pursuit of Piety by the Reverend John Wesley and the Reverend Charles Wesley

John and Charles Wesley were raised in a Christian home at Epworth by their parents Samuel and Susanna Wesley. Susanna trained them from their infancy to form good habits. John Wesley asked her what principal rules were observed in educating her children, she replied to him in her letter dated July 24, 1732:

> The children were always put into a regular method of living, in such things as they were capable of, from their birth; as in dressing, undressing, changing their linen, &c.

> When turned a year old (and some before) they were taught to fear the rod, and cry softly; by which means they escaped abundance of correction they might otherwise have had;

> In order to form the minds of children, the first thing to be done is to conquer their will, and bring them to an obedient temper. To inform the understanding is a work of time, and must with children proceed by slow degrees as they are able to bear it; but subjecting the will, is a thing which must be done at once; and the sooner the better.

> For by neglecting timely correction, they will contract a stubbornness
> and obstinacy, which is hardly ever after conquered; and never, without
> using such severity as would be as painful to me as to the child...
>
> I insist upon conquering the will of children betimes, because this is the
> only strong and rational foundation of a religious education; without
> which both precept and example will be ineffectual. But when this is
> thoroughly done, then the child is capable of being governed by the reason
> and piety of its parents, till its own understanding comes to maturity,
> and the principles of religion have taken root in the mind.
>
> I cannot yet dismiss this subject. As selfwill is the root of all sin and misery,
> so whatever cherishes this in children, insures their after wretchedness
> and irreligion: Whatever checks and mortifies it, promotes their future
> happiness and piety. This is still more evident, if we farther consider, that
> religion is nothing else than doing the will of God, and not our own: That
> the one grand impediment to our temporal and eternal happiness being
> this selfwill, no indulgence of it can be trivial, no denial unprofitable.
> Heaven or hell depends on this alone. So that the parent who studies
> to subdue it in his child, works together with God in the renewing and
> saving a soul. The parent who indulge it does the devil's work, makes
> religion impracticable, salvation unattainable; and does all that in him
> lies to damn his child, soul and body for ever.[11]

John Wesley matriculated at Christ Church College, Oxford in 1720 and
graduated with a B. A. in 1724 from Oxford University. He had to choose
a career in 1725 out of the three learned professions: the law, medicine
or the church. The forces of heredity, the pressure of his training, and
qualities of his natural temperament carried him in the direction of a
church ministry. His father was pressing him in the same direction.[12]
His decision to take Holy Orders made him to think about the ministry
seriously and realize that he was not spiritually fit for the work of the
ministry. He described his spiritual condition in these words:

> Being removed to the University for five years, I still said my prayers
> both in public and in private, and read, with the Scriptures, several
> other books of religion, especially comments on the New Testament.
> Yet I had not all this while so much as a notion of inward holiness; nay,
> went on habitually, and for the most part very contentedly, in some one
> or other known sin, though with some intermission and short struggles,
> especially before and after the Holy Communion which I was obliged to
> receive thrice a year.[13]

While he was thinking of his unfitness for the ministry, he met a porter of his college; they had the following conversation:

John: Go home and get another coat.

Porter: This is the only coat I have in the world, and I thank God for it.

John: Go home and get your supper, then.

Porter: I have had nothing today but a drink of water, and I thank God for that.

John: It is late, and you will be locked out, and then what will you have to thank God for?

Porter: I will thank him that I have the dry stones to lie upon.

John: John [Porter], you thank God when you have nothing to wear, nothing to eat, and no bed to lie upon, what else do you thank him for?

Porter: I thank him that he has given me my life and being, a heart to love him, and desire to serve him.[14]

These words and the tone of the porter made John Wesley feel that there was something in religion which he had not yet found and he had to find it out diligently.

John Wesley wrote to his parents concerning his decision to enter the ministry. His father wanted of him to have a proper motive to enter the ministry. He wrote:

My thoughts are: if it is no harm to desire getting into that office, even as Eli's sons, to eat a piece of bread, yet certainly a desire and an intention to lead a stricter life, and a belief that one should do so, is a better reason. Though this should by all means be begun before, or ten to one it will deceive us afterwards.[15]

His mother also wrote him:

I, who am apt to be sanguine, hope it may proceed from the operation of God's Holy Spirit, that by taking away your relish of sensual enjoyments He may prepare and dispose your mind for a more serious and close application to things of a more sublime and spiritual nature. If it be so, happy are you if you cherish those dispositions, and now in good earnest resolve to make religion the business of your life...Now I mention this, it calls to mind your letter to your father about taking Orders. I was much pleased with it, and liked the proposal well... I approve the disposition of your mind and think the sooner you are a deacon the better; because it may be an inducement to greater application in the study of practical divinity, which I humbly conceive is the best study for candidates for Orders.[16]

John Wesley earnestly began to prepare himself for the new career as a minister; he selected books on devotion by Thomas `a Kempis (1380-1471), Jeremy Taylor (1613-1667), and William Law (1686-1761). Those serious minded writers influenced Wesley very much. He first read *Imitation of Christ* or *The Christian's Pattern* by Thomas `a Kempis. This book had been his father's favorite book, as a "great and old champion."[17]

John Wesley wrote how the book influenced him to change his religious life:

> When I was about twentytwo, my father pressed me to enter into holy orders. At the same time, the providence of God directing me to Kempis's "*Christian Pattern*," I began to see, that true religion was seated in the heart, and that God's law extended to all our thoughts as well words and actions. I was, however, very angry at Kempis, for being too strict; though I read him only in Dean Stanhope's translation. Yet I had frequently much sensible comfort in reading him, such as I was an utter stranger before: And meeting likewise with a religious friend, which I never had till now, I began to alter the whole form of my conversation, and to set in earnest upon a new life. I set apart an hour or two a day for religious retirement. I communicated every week. I watched against all sin, whether in word or deed. I began to aim at, and pray for, inward holiness. So that now, 'doing so much, and living so good a life,' I doubted not but I was a good Christian.[18]

John Wesley wrote this account in his journal on Wednesday, May 24, 1738. But when he wrote papers on "A Plain Account of Christian Perfection," he wrote that he met with Kempis's "*Christian's Pattern*" in 1726.[19] There he acknowledged how Kempis helped him to pursue Christian piety. He wrote:

> The nature and extent of inward religion, the religion of the heart, now appeared to me in a stronger light than ever it had done before. I saw, that giving even all my life to God (supposing it possible to do this, and go

on farther) would profit me nothing, unless I gave my heart, yea, all my heart to him. I saw, that 'simplicity of intention, and purity of affection,' one design in all we speak or do, and one desire ruling all our tempers, are indeed 'the wings of the soul,' without which she can never ascend to the mount of God.[20]

Then John Wesley read Bishop Jeremy Taylor's book, *Rule and Exercises of Holy Living and Dying*, when he was twenty-three. This book strengthened the religious conviction of Wesley which was awakened by Kempis.[21] Wesley stated how this book influenced him:

In reading several parts of this book, I was exceedingly affected; that part in particular which relates to purity of intention. Instantly I resolved to dedicate all my life to God, all my thoughts, and words, and actions; being thoroughly convinced, there was no medium; but that every part of my life (not some only) must either be a sacrifice to God, or myself, that is, in effect, to the devil.Can any serious person doubt of this, or find a medium between serving God and serving the devil?[22]

Having read *Imitation of Christ* or *Christian's Pattern* of Kempis and *Rule and Exercises of Holy Living and Dying* of Bishop Taylor, John Wesley was prepared for the holy order of Deacon. He was ordained a deacon by John Potter, Bishop of Oxford on Sunday, September 19, 1725. He was elected a fellow of Lincoln College in 1726. This position brought him financial relief. It was an answer to his mother's prayer.

At Lincoln College, he read William Law's *A Serious Call to a Devout and Holy Life* and *Christian Perfection*, while he was watching more carefully against actual sins and advising others to be religious. He was influenced by these two books. He wrote in his journal, May 24, 1738:

But meeting now with Mr. Law's "*Christian Perfection*" and "*Serious Call,*" although I was much offended at many parts of both, yet they convinced me more than ever of the exceeding height and breadth and depth of the law of God. The light flowed in so mightily upon my soul, that every thing appeared in a new view. I cried to God for help, and resolved not to prolong the time of obeying Him as I had never done before. And by my continued endeavour to keep His whole law, inward and outward, to the utmost of my power, I was persuaded that I should be accepted of Him, and that I was even then in a state of salvation.[23]

By reading these books he was convinced of the absolute impossibility of being half Christian and he determined to be all devoted to God and to give God his all soul, body, and substance.[24]

John Wesley received his M. A. in 1727 from Oxford University. In August 1727, he became his father's curate at Epworth and Wroote. He was ordained a priest on September 22, 1728 by Bishop John Potter of Oxford. He served in this capacity until November 22, 1729, when he was called to Oxford to be a Moderator; he remained at Oxford until October 6, 1735, when he left for Georgia.[25]

While John Wesley was serving as a curate at Wroote, he met a serious man, who said to John Wesley:

> Sir, you wish to serve God and go to heaven. Remember you cannot serve him alone; you must therefore find companions or make them; the Bible knows nothing of solitary religion.[26]

Beginning of Methodism

While John Wesley was at Lincoln College in 1726, his brother Charles joined Christ Church College. John asked him to be pious but Charles resisted his brother's attempt. John went to Wroote to assist his father as curator. Charles took his studies seriously. His serious thinking led him to participate the Lord's supper every week. He induced other students to unite with him in seeking true holiness. This led to form a club. Charles wrote to John in a changed mood:

> There is no one person I would so willingly have to be the instrument of good to me as you. It is owing, in great measure, to somebody's prayers (my mother's most likely) that I am come to think as I do; for I cannot tell myself how or why I awoke out of my lethargy, only that it was not long after you went away.[27]

When the club was formed, Charles and his companions adopted some rules for right living; they apportioned time to study, religious duties, and devotion. The club members took all duties seriously. They kept the Law of God, rule of the Church, statute of the University with exact precision. These were startling novelties. The public took notice of them and they wittily gave various labels to the club, such as, 'Godly Club,' 'Holy Club,' 'Bible moths,' 'Bible Bigots,' 'Sacramentarians', 'Supererogation Men,' and 'Methodist.'[28] It was the youthful wit which invented the label 'Methodist.' Charles Wesley told why the name "Methodist" was given to his group as he said that the name "Methodist" was bestowed upon himself and his friends because of their strict conformity to the method of study prescribed by the university.[29]

John Wesley was called by Christ Church College to be a Moderator on November 29, 1729. He joined the club and became its leading spirit. Mr. Charles Wesley, Mr. Morgan, Mr. Kirkham and Mr. John Wesley were the four gentlemen of Oxford who formed the club. This was the first rise of Methodism. John stamped an even deeper seriousness on the life of the club and added new religious duties to the club. The club began to meet every night to review what had been done and to plan activities of the next day. They visited the sick, helped the poor, taught the children in the school, and visited the inmates in prison.[30] He was styled the "Father of the Holy Club."[31] When Samuel Wesley heard the new title of his son, he wrote:

> If this be so, I am sure I am the grandfather of it; and I need not say that I had rather any of sons should be so dignified and distinguished than to have the title of 'His Holiness.'[32]

John Wesley stated that he began to be *homo unius libri* (a man of one book) in 1730. He began to study(comparatively) no book but the Bible. Then he saw in a brighter light than before that he needed the faith which expresses his love to God and man and works inward and outward holiness. He decided to love God with all his heart to serve Him with all his strength.[33] Each of the other clubmembers was *homo unius libri*.[34] They were searching the Bible with earnestness and openmindedness. The Bible was the only one rule of their judgment. The club carried out spiritual and humanitarian activities but it remained scriptural throughout. This was the fundamental fact of the rise of Methodism; and it should not be forgotten at any time.

As the "holy club" made the Bible as the only basis of their judgment, the club began to take theological stands on many issues. It rejected some beliefs and practices of the Roman Catholic Church and the Calvinistic doctrine of predestination. It suffices to say that when the movement, led by the Wesley brothers, became an established church as Methodist Church, the church formed its twenty-five articles of religion on the basis of the Bible.

Samuel Wesley died on April 25, 1735; his sons, John and Charles, were by his bedside during his last hours. He said to John, "The inward witness, son, the inward witness this is the proof, the strongest proof of Christianity."[35] John had to understand these words in the future. Charles Wesley was ordained deacon and, shortly after, priest in 1735.

John Wesley, Charles Wesley, Benjamin Ingham, and Charles Delamotte, these four members of the holy club left for Georgia on October 14, 1735. John Wesley met a Moravian pastor, Spangenberg on the ship, who asked John these two questions, on February 7, 1736: "Have you the witness within yourself? Does the Spirit of God witness with your spirit that you are [a] child of God? "John did not know what to answer. [36] These questions made him to remind of the last words of his father, "the inward witness, son, the inward witness" and to feel the need of personal conviction of being saved.

The missionary work of John Wesley in Georgia gave the second rise of Methodism, when in April 1736 his twenty or thirty parishioners met at his house for prayers, singing, and mutual exhortation on Saturday evenings and other evenings. This format of the prayer meeting formed the "first rudiments of the Methodist Society." [37] Nevertheless, the work of Wesley brothers in America was not a success. Charles Wesley returned to England in 1736. John Wesley returned to England on February 1, 1738, and entered in his journal:

> 'Why (...) that I who went to America to convert others was never myself converted to God.' The faith I want is....' A sure trust and confidence in God, that, through the merits of Christ, my sins are forgiven, and I reconciled to the favour of God.'[38]

John Wesley met Peter Bohler(1712-1775), another Moravian missionary in England, who influenced John very much and who convinced John of his unbelief on March 5,1738. Wesley wrote in his journal about their meeting, "Bohler amazed me more and more by the account he gave of fruits of faith, the love, holiness, and happiness that he affirmed to attend it."[39] John Wesley accepted Bohler's teaching. Bohler advised Wesley, "Preach faith till you have it; and then because you have it, you will preach faith."[40]

John Wesley went very unwillingly to a society in Nettleton Court on Aldersgate Street on May 14, 1738. Someone was reading Martin Luther's (1483-1546) Preface to the Epistle to the Romans. In that meeting Wesley had the experience of his personal conversion. He recorded:

> About a quarter before nine, while he was describing the change which God works in the heart through faith in Christ. I felt my heart strangely warmed. I felt I did trust in Christ, Christ alone, for salvation: And an assurance was given me that he had taken away my sins, even mine, and saved me from the law of sin and death.[41]

John Wesley's conversion revolutionized his character and the method of his preaching. On June 11, 1738, eight days after his conversion, he preached his famous sermon before the University of Oxford on "By grace are ye saved through faith"; this was the keynote of his entire ministry.[42]

Charles Wesley also met Peter Bohler on April 20, 1738. They discussed whether conversion was gradual or instantaneous in the presence of John Wesley. A week later, Charles was very sick on 28th April. Bohler stood by his bedside and prayed that Charles might see the divine intervention in Bohler's being detained. Charles confessed his unbelief and lack of forgiveness to Bohler. Charles had a long discussion with Bohler. The discussion opened the eyes of Charles to the true nature of living faith, whereby alone, "through grace, we are saved." Bohler left for Carolina on the next day.[43] Bohler was replaced by John Bray. He prayed with Charles. A devout woman, who was assisting in nursing Charles, was seized with the conviction that she ought to speak some words of comfort to Charles. She said to him, "In the name of Christ of Nazareth, arise! Thou shall be healed of all thy infirmities."[44] Charles was healed and his strength returned to him and he had found rest to his soul. John Wesley was given this good news on Sunday, May 21, 1738.[45]

After the conversion of John Wesley, there was a third rise of Methodist society on May 1, 1738 in London at FetterLane when forty or fifty members of the society agreed to meet together on every Wednesday evening for prayers, conversation, and singing.[46]

Ways to Enforce Social Morality

At the third rise of Methodism on May 1, 1739, the society made the following fundamental rules in accordance with the scripture (The Letter of St. James) and advice of Peter Bohler:

1. That we meet together once a week to "confess our faults one to another, and pray one for another, that we may be healed.

2. That the persons so meeting be divided into several bands, or little companies, none of them consisting of fewer than five, or more than ten persons.

3. That every one in order to speak as freely, plainly, and concisely as he can, the real estate of his heart, with his several temptations and deliverances, since the last time of meeting.

4. That all the bands have a conference at eight every Wednesday evening, begun and ended with singing and prayer.

5. That any one who desires to be admitted into the society be asked, "What are your reasons for desiring this? Will you be entirely open, using no kind of reserve? Have you any objection to any of our orders?" (which may then be read.)

6. That when any new member is proposed, every one present speak clearly and freely whatever objection he has to him.

7. That those against whom no reasonable objection appears, he, in order for their trial, formed into one or more distinct bands, and some person agreed on to assist them.

8. That after two months' trial, if no objection appear, they may be admitted into the society.

9. That every fourth Saturday be observed as a day of general intercession.

10. That on the Sunday seven, night following be a general lovefeast, from seven till ten in the evening.

11. That no particular member be allowed to act in any thing contrary to any order of the society: And that if any persons, after being thrice admonished, do not conform thereto, they be not any longer esteemed as members.[47]

These rules were meant to maintain both personal and collective piety of the group in the following manners. First, each person was expected to confess his faults and wrong doings to the band; they were praying together to get God's help to be healed spiritually. The band had to meet every Wednesday evening for singing and prayer. Secondly, the process of admission of the new members into the band was thorough and cautious; the new members were examined of their motives to join the band; if there was an objection against any new member, he was not admitted in the band; the new members, against whom was no objection, were put on trial for two months. Thirdly, if a member of the band or society acted against any rule of the society, he was admonished. After the third admonishment, he was removed from the membership of the society.

The societies began to grow rapidly. Its membership was scattered so wide that John Wesley could not see the behaviour of all members. A new method was invented by a circumstance. There was a large debt on the meetinghouse in Bristol; Wesley called the main men for consultation in 1742. Captain Foy suggested that every member of the society give a penny a week till all the debt is paid. Thus, the penny fund was established to solve the financial problem. While money was being collected, some persons reported to John Wesley that some were not living life as they ought. This led Wesley to think of a plan by which the spiritual welfare of every member might be secured. He called all the leaders of classes and asked them to make inquiry into the behaviour of those they visited. By this, many disorderly persons were detected. Some turned from the evil of their ways; others were put out of the society. This was the way of maintaining discipline.[48]

On February 23, 1743, John Wesley sent forth the General Rules in his own name and on May 1, 1743, Charles Wesley's name was added to the same pamphlet. In that publication, the society was defined as "a company of men, having the form and seeking the power of godliness, united in order to pray together, to receive the word of exhortation, and to watch over one another in love, that they may help each other to work out their salvation." The condition for admission into the societies was "desire to flee from the wrath to come, and to be saved from their sins." The members were expected to evidence their desire of salvation by following things: (i) doing no harm, (ii) avoiding evil in every kind, and specially such diversions as cannot be used in the name of the Lord Jesus, (iii) doing good of every kind to all men, (iv) attending all ordinances of God such as public worship, Lord's Supper, family and private prayer, searching the scripture, fasting, and abstinence.[49]

John Wesley began to pay quarterly visit to classes and preachers and issue a ticket of membership in 1742. Wesley wrote about this practice, "To each of those of whose seriousness and good conversation I found no reason to doubt, I gave a testimony under my own hand, by writing their name on a ticket prepared for that purpose; every ticket implying as strong recommendation of the person to whom it was given as if I had written at length, 'I believe the bearer hereof to be one that fears God and works righteousness.'" He added that issuing a quarterly ticket served as a quiet and inoffensive method of removing any disorderly member from the fellowship of the society.[50]

Wesley also revived the early church's love feast (*agape*) and celebrated it at every quarterly meeting.[51] He also introduced "covenant with God" service since 1747 so that Methodists maintain their piety and commitment to God's work.[52]

Scriptural Holiness of Methodism

John Wesley was a theologian and a preacher. His brother Charles was a preacher and a hymnwriter. Through their works, they defined Christian principles and practices for the people called Methodists.

It was pointed out that the founders of the Methodism made the Bible, the scripture, as the ultimate authority in defining and determining what are the true religious principles and practices of Christianity. The belief of Methodism in the written word of God to be the only and sufficient rule both for Christian faith and practice made Methodism fundamentally different from the Roman Catholic Church.[53] In defense of Methodism, John Wesley wrote:

> What was their [of Methodists] fundamental doctrine? That the Bible is the whole and sole rule both of Christian faith and practice. Hence they learned, (1) That religion is an inward principle; that it is no other than the mind that was in Christ; or, in other words, the renewal of the soul after the image of God, in righteousness and true holiness.
>
> (2) That this can never be wrought in us, but by the power of the Holy Ghost.
>
> (3) That we receive this, and every other blessing, merely for the sake of Christ. And
>
> (4) That whosoever hath the mind that was in Christ, the same is our brother, and sister, and mother.[54]

Commenting on the history of Methodism, John Wesley said that the founders of Methodism were downright "Bible Christians" to whom the Bible was the whole and sole rule and their intention was to preach old, Bible Christianity.[55] Those Bible Christians were given the name "Methodists."[56]

In his article, "The character of a Methodist," John Wesley defined who is Methodist. He wrote:

A Methodist is one who has 'the love of God shed abroad in his heart by the Holy ghost given unto him;' one who loves the Lord his God with all his heart, and with all his soul and with all his mind, and with all his strength.[57]

A Methodist loves God with all his heart and serves God with all his strength, said Wesley.[58] In concluding the article, Wesley again defined who is Methodist, saying:

He is a Christian, not in name only, but in heart and in life. He is inwardly and outwardly conformed to the will of God, as revealed in the written word. He thinks, speaks, and lives, according to the method laid down in the revelation of Jesus Christ. His soul is renewed after the image of God, in righteousness and in all true holiness. And having the mind that was in Christ, he so walks as Christ also walked.[59]

In his another article, "Advice to the People Called Methodist," he defined Methodist as a believer practicing inward and outward holiness, in these words:

By Methodists I mean, a people who profess to pursue (in whatever measure they have attained) holiness of heart and life, inward and outward conformity in all things, to the revealed will of God; who place religion in an uniform resemblance of the great object of it; in a steady imitation of Him they worship, in all his imitable perfections; more particularly, in justice, mercy, and truth, or universal love filling the heart, and governing the life.[60]

The above cited definitions about Methodist can be summarized that a Methodist loves God with all his heart and serves God wholeheartedly; he practices inward and outward holiness; his soul is renewed in the image of God and he imitates Jesus Christ; he practices justice, mercy, truth and universal love in his life. In short, he is a spiritual child of God in the light of the scripture. Therefore his religion, which is Methodism, is a scriptural Christianity. John Wesley, in his article, "The Principles of a Methodist Farther Explained, defined the religion of Methodists in these words:

'The loving God with all our heart, and our neighbour as ourselves; and in that love abstaining from all evil, and doing all possible good to all men.'

The same meaning we have sometimes expressed a little more at large, thus:

> 'Religion we conceive to be no other than love; the love of God and of all mankind; the loving God 'with all our heart, and soul, and strength,' as having 'first loved us,' as the fountain of all the good we have received, and of all we ever hope to enjoy; and the loving every soul which God hath made, every man on earth, as our own soul.[61]

In other words, Methodist religion is also universal Christianity.

A commission of the Methodist Church is to spread the scriptural Christianity in the world. John Wesley wrote about it saying:

> This religion we long to see established in the world, a religion of love, and joy, and peace; having its seat in the heart, in the inmost soul, but ever showing itself by its fruits; continually springing forth, not only in all innocence, (for love worketh no ill to his neighbour,) but likewise in every kind of beneficence, spreading virtue and happiness all around it.[62]

In a similar way, the commission of the Methodist Church is stated in "The Order of service for the Public Reception (Confirmation) of New Members" as follows:

> Within the Christian Church One, Holy, Catholic and Apostolic the Methodist Church holds and cherishes a true place, having been raised by God to spread Scriptural Holiness throughout the world.[63]

The commission of the Methodist is to spread the scriptural holiness or a biblical religion in the world. John Wesley had defined what is 'Methodism' and who are 'Methodists' in terms of religious principles of faith and practices, which make inward and outward holiness for Christians called Methodists.

Let us now think of the questions such as: Did John Wesley differ from the concepts of holiness which were professed by other Christian bodies? And what was the main reason of his different stand?

John Wesley, in his article, "A Short View of the Difference Between the Moravian Brethren, (so called,) and the Rev. Mr. John and Charles Wesley," first stated the propositions of Moravian doctrine and then said that the first of those propositions was ambiguous and the rest [remaining six] were utterly false.

" 1. Christ has done all that was necessary for the salvation of all mankind."

This is ambiguous. Christ has not done all which was necessary for the absolute salvation of all mankind. For notwithstanding all that Christ has done, he that believeth not shall be damned. But he has done all which was necessary for the conditional salvation of all mankind; that is, if they believe; for through his merits all that believe to the end, with the faith that worketh by love, shall be saved.[64]

Wesley stated the fourth proposition of the Moravian doctrine as follows:

"4. That Christ has taken away all other commands and duties, having wholly 'abolished the law;' that a believer is therefore 'free from the law,' is not obliged thereby to do or omit anything; it being inconsistent with his liberty to do anything as commanded."

Wesley commented on this proposition saying:

How absolutely contrary is this to his own solemn declaration! 'Think not that I have come to destroy the law or the Prophets. I am not come to destroy, but to fulfil. One jot or one title shall in nowise pass from the law, till heaven and earth pass.'[65]

Wesley differed from the Moravians on the basis of the scripture.

Commenting on the later part of the proposition, referring to the liberty from the law, John Wesley said:

So your liberty is a liberty to disobey God; whereas ours is a liberty to obey him in all things: So grossly, while we 'establish the law do you make void the law through faith!'[66]

Wesley stated the sixth proposition of the Moravian doctrine, referring to the concept of holiness, as follows:

"6. That a believer is never sanctified or holy in himself, but in Christ only; he has no holiness in himself at all, all his holiness being imputed, not inherent."

Wesley differed from the position as he argued:

> Scripture holiness is the image of God; the mind which was in Christ; the love of God and man; lowliness, gentleness, temperance, patience, chastity. And do you coolly affirm, that this is only imputed to a believer, and that he has none at all of this holiness in him? Is temperance imputed only to him that is a drunkard still; or chastity, to her that goes on in whoredom? Nay, but a believer is really chaste and temperate. And if so, he is thus far holy in himself.[67]

In these words, Wesley defined the scriptural holiness which includes both inward and outward holiness. And inward holiness and outward holiness go hand in hand one with the other.

John Wesley did not approve of anyone preaching Christianity devoid of holiness or turning the grace of God into lasciviousness. He took a stand against a supposed teaching of Simon Magus. Simon was a magician and he wanted to buy the power of the Holy Spirit to heal and do miracles, from apostle Peter. Peter opposed Simon Magus (Acts 8:9-24). Simon Magus was the first of the heretics.[68]

Simon Magus supposedly taught:

> that Christ had done, as well as suffered, all; that his righteousness being imputed to us, we need none of our own; that seeing there was so much righteousness and holiness in Him, there needs none in us; that to think we have any, or to desire or seek any, is to renounce Christ; that from the beginning to the end of salvation, all is in Christ, nothing in man; and that those who teach other wise are legal Preachers, and know nothing of the gospel.[69]

Simon Magus's teaching was same as that of the Moravians. John Wesley in his article, "A Blow at the Root; or Christ Stabbed in the House of His Friend," firmly responded saying:

> This is indeed 'a blow at the root,' the root of all holiness, all true religion. Hereby Christ is 'stabbed in the house of his friends,' of those who make the largest professions of loving and honouring him; the whole design of his death, namely, 'to destroy the works of the devil,' being overthrown at a stroke. For wherever this doctrine is cordially received, it leaves no place of holiness. It demolishes it from top to bottom; it destroys both root and branch. It effectually tears up all desire of it, all endeavour after

> it. It forbids all such exhortations as might excite those desires or awaken those endeavours. Nay, it makes men afraid of personal holiness, afraid of cherishing any thought of it, or motion toward it, lest they should deny the faith, and reject Christ and his righteousness: So that, instead of being 'zealous of good works,' they are a stink in their nostrils. And they are infinitely more afraid of 'the works of God,' than of 'the works of the devil.'

> Here is the masterpiece of Satan ....Men are holy, without a grain of holiness in them! holy in Christ, however unholy in themselves; they are in Christ, without one jot of the mind that was in Christ; in Christ, though their nature is whole in them. They are 'complete in him,' though they are, in themselves, as proud, as vain, as covetous, as passionate as ever. It is enough.[70]

Having evaluated the teaching of Simon Magus, John Wesley appealed to Christians saying:

> 'O ye simple ones, how long will you love simplicity?' How long will ye 'seek death in the error of your life?' 'Know ye not, 'whoever teacheth you otherwise,' that the unrighteous shall not inherit the kingdom of God?' 'Be not deceived;' although there are many lie in wait to deceive, and that under the fair pretense of exalting Christ; a pretense which the more easily steals upon you, because 'to you he is precious.' But as the Lord liveth, 'neither fornicators, nor idolaters, nor adulterers, nor effeminate, nor sodomites, nor thieves, nor covetous, nor drunkards, nor revilers, nor extortioners, shall inherit the kingdom of God.' [I Cor. 6:610][71]

As Simon Magus was teaching false liberty, John Wesley defined the true liberty for Christians saying, "This is true liberty, true gospel liberty, experienced by every believer: Not freedom from the law of God, or the works of God, but from the law of sin and the works of the devil." Then he exhorted them saying:

> I testify unto you, that if you still continue in sin, Christ shall profit you nothing; that Christ is not Saviour to you, unless he saves you from your sins; and that unless it purify your heart, faith shall profit you nothing. O when will ye understand, that to oppose either inward or outward holiness, under colour of exalting Christ, is directly to act the part of Judas, to 'betray the Son of man with a kiss.'[72]

John Wesley in his sermon xxv, "Upon Our Lord's Sermon on the Mount Discourse v" argued the relationship between the Gospel of Jesus Christ and the Law of the Old Testament. He chose the text, Matthew 5:17-20 and advanced his argument on each verse. He wrote:

> And First, "Think not I am come to destroy the Law, or the Prophets: I am not come to destroy, but to fulfill."

> The ritual or ceremonial law, delivered by Moses to the children of Israel, containing all the injunctions and ordinances which related to the old sacrifices and service of the Temple, our Lord indeed come to destroy, to dissolve, and utterly abolish. To this bear all the Apostles witness; not only Barnabas and Paul, who vehemently withstood those who taught that Christians 'ought to keep the law of Moses;' (Acts xv.5;) not only St. Peter, who termed the insisting on this, on the observance of the ritual law, a 'tempting God,' and 'putting a yoke upon the neck of the disciples, which neither our fathers,' saith he, 'nor we, were able to bear;' but all the Apostles, elders, and brethren, being assembled with one accord, (verse 22,) declared that to command them to keep this law, was to 'subvert their souls;' and that 'it seemed good to the Holy Ghost' and to them, to lay no such burden upon them. This 'handwriting of ordinances our Lord did blot out, take away, and nail to his cross.' (Verse 28)[73]

Having argued that the Lord Jesus Christ blotted out the ceremonial or ritual law, on the basis of the scripture, John Wesley then made a distinction between the ceremonial law and the moral law which was not blotted out. He said:

> But the moral law, contained in the Ten Commandments, and enforced by the Prophets, he [Lord Jesus Christ] did not take away. It was not the design of his coming to revoke any part of this.

> This is a law which never can be broken, which 'stands fast as the faithful witness in heaven.' The moral law stands on an entirely different foundation from the ceremonial or ritual law....Every part of this law must remain in force upon all mankind, and in all ages; as not depending either on time or place, or any other circumstances liable to change, but on the nature of God, and the nature of man, and their unchangeable relation to each other.[74]

John Wesley quoted the next verse: "For verily I say unto you," (a solemn preface, which denotes both the importance and certainty of what is spoken,) "till heaven and earth pass, one jot or one title shall in no wise pass from the law, till all be fulfilled."

Commenting on the words "one jot," he wrote:

> It is a proverbial expression, which signifies that no one commandment contained in the moral law, nor the least part of any one, however inconsiderable it might seem shall be disannuled. He then added saying, "It is a word of authority, expressing the sovereign will and power of Him that spake; of Him whose word is the law of heaven and earth, and stands fast for ever and ever." He brought out the implied relationship between the gospel and the moral law saying, "From all this we may learn, that there is no contrariety at all between the law and the gospel; that there is no need for the law to pass away, in order to establish the gospel. Indeed neither of them supersedes the other, but they agree perfectly well together....There is, therefore, the closest connexion that can be conceived, between the law and the gospel. On the one hand, the law continually makes way for, and points us to, the gospel; on the other, the gospel continually leads us to a more exact fulfilling of the law.[75]

John Wesley, in his sermon CXX, "On the Wedding Garment," stressed the necessity of holiness. He argued:

> Does not that expression, 'the righteousness of the saints,' point out what is the 'wedding garment' in the parable? It is the 'holiness without which no man shall see the Lord.' The righteousness of Christ is doubtless necessary for any soul that enters into glory: But so is personal holiness too, for every child of man. But it is highly needful to be observed, that they are necessary in different respects. The former is necessary to entitle us to heaven; the latter to qualify us for it. Without the righteousness of Christ we could have no claim to glory; without holiness we could have no fitness for it. By the former we become members of Christ, children of God and heirs of the kingdom of heaven. By the latter 'we are made meet to be partakers of the inheritance of the saints in light.'[76]

Rev. Charles Wesley was a hymnwriter. Through his hymns he preached scriptural Christianity and holiness. In the preface to *Selection of Hymns from the 1780 Handbook*, he wrote:

> As but a small part of these hymns are of my composing. I do not think it inconsistent with modesty to declare that I am persuaded no such hymn book as this has yet been published in the English language. In what other publication of the kind have you so distinct and full an account of scriptural Christianity? ... And so clear direction for making our calling and election sure, for perfecting holiness in the fear of God?[77]

Charles Wesley, like his brother John, spoke about the inward and outward piety or holiness in his hymns. Let us look at his few hymns:

What is our calling's glorious hope

But inward holiness?

For this to Jesus I look up,

I calmly wait for this.

I wait, till he shall touch me clean,

Shall life and power impart;

Gives me the faith that casts out sin,

And purifies the heart.

This is the dear redeeming grace,

For every sinner free;

Surely it shall on me take place,

The chief of sinners, me.

From all iniquity, from all,

He shall my soul redeem:

In Jesus I believe, and shall

Believe myself to him.

When Jesus makes my heart his home,

My sin shall all depart:

And lo! he saith, I quickly come,

To fill and rule thy heart.

Be it according to thy word!

Redeem me from all sin;

My heart would now receive thee, Lord:

Come in, my Lord, come in![78]

In another hymn, Charles Wesley talked about the inward and outward holiness.

> Be it my only wisdom here,
>
> To serve the Lord with filial fear,
>
> With loving gratitude;
>
> Superior sense may I display
>
> By shunning every evil way,
>
> And walking in the good.
>
> Oh, may I still from sin depart;
>
> A wise and understanding heart,
>
> Jesus, to me be given!
>
> And let me through thy Spirit know
>
> To glorify my God below,
>
> And find my way to heaven.[79]

Theological propositions which were upheld by Wesley brothers are confirmed by modern writers such as John Charles Ryle and Jerry Bridges. J. C. Ryle in the introduction of his book '*Holiness: Its Nature, Hindrances, Difficulties, and Roots*' says that the cause of scriptural holiness is an exciting and interesting cause in the present time and his work is a contribution toward advancing kingdom of Christ in the world.[80] In this book, he agrees with Wesley brothers as he wrote:

> For one thing, we must be holy, because the voice of God in the scripture plainly commands it. The Lord Jesus says to His people, 'Except your righteousness shall exceed the righteousness of the scribes and Pharisees, ye shall in no case enter the kingdom of heaven' (Matt, 5:20). 'Be ye .... perfect, even as your Father which is in heaven is perfect' (Matt. 5:48) Paul tells the Thessalonians, 'This is the will of God, even your sanctification' (I Thes. 4:3). And Peter says, 'As He which hath called you is holy, so be ye holy in all manner of conversation; because it is written, "Be ye holy, for I am holy " (1 Peter 1:15, 16). 'In this,' says Leighton, 'law and gospel agree.'[81]

He emphasizes the necessity both of inward and outward holiness, as Wesley brothers did, when he wrote,

We must not merely have a Christian name and Christian knowledge, we must have a Christian character also. We must be saints on earth, if ever we mean to be saints in heaven. God has said it and He will not go back: 'Without holiness no man shall see the Lord.'...'Let not men deceive themselves,' says Owen, 'sanctification is a qualification indispensably necessary unto those who will be under the conduct of the Lord Christ unto salvation. He leads none to heaven but whom He sanctifies on the earth...'[82]

Commenting on Hebrews 12:14, "Make every effort to live in peace with all men and to be holy; without holiness no one will see the Lord," J. Bridges wrote about two aspects of holiness, as follows:

Scripture speaks of both a holiness which we have in Christ before God, and a holiness which we are to strive after. These two aspects of holiness complement one another, for our salvation is a salvation to holiness: 'For God did not call us to be impure, but to live a holy life' (1 Thessalonians 4:7). To the Corinthians Paul wrote: 'To the church of God at Corinth, to those sanctified in Christ Jesus and called to be holy' (1 Corinthians 1:2). The word sanctified here means 'made holy'. That is, we are through Christ made holy in our standing before God, and called to be holy in our daily lives.

So the writer of Hebrews is telling us to take seriously the necessity of personal, practical holiness. When the Holy Spirit comes into our lives at our salvation, he comes to make us holy in practice.[83]

Conclusion

Both male and female ancestors and the parents of John and Charles Wesley had pietistic background which helped John and Charles to practice and preach the scriptural holiness. Books of Thomas a Kempis, Jeremy Taylor, and William Law influenced John Wesley to pursue the path of holiness in his life. Charles also followed the path as his brother John.

Their seriousness of life made them to take Christian life seriously. They advocated their life style to others. They made the Bible as the sole authority of their life and theology. They formed a 'holy society or club' which was also called Methodism.

When Methodism was spreading in England and America, they enforced some rules and introduced other ways for their societies to uphold scriptural holiness.

Endnotes

[1] A Methodist Preacher, *John Wesley the Methodist: A Plain Account of His Life and Work*, (New York: Eaton & Mains, 1903), p. 11.

[2] Rev. W. H. Fitchett, *Wesley and His Century: A Study in Spiritual Forces*, (Toronto: The Ryerson Press, 1920), p. 13.

[3] A Methodist Preacher, op. cit., p. 14.

[4] A Methodist Preacher, op.cit. p. 19.

[5] Ibid., p. 20.

[6] *A Methodist Preacher*, op.cit., pp. 22 23, 16.

[7] Ibid., pp. 23 24.

[8] A Methodist Preacher op.cit., p. 24.

[9] Ibid., p. 139.

[10] Ibid. p. 38.

[11] *The Works of John Wesley*,(Grand Rapids, Michigan: Baker Book House,3rd ed., 1984), Vol. I, pp. 387 389.

[12] W. H. Fitchett, op. cit., p.61.

[13] *The Works of John Wesley*, Vol. I, p. 98; A Methodist Preacher, op.cit., 55.

[14] A Methodist Preacher, op.cit., p. 55.

[15] W. H. Fitchett, op. cit., p. 62.

[16]W. H. Fitchett, op.cit., p. 62.

[17] A Methodist Preacher, op. cit., p. 57.

[18] *The Works of John Wesley*, Vol. I, p. 99.

[19] Ibid., Vol. XI, p. 366.

[20] *The Works of John Wesley*. Vol. XI., pp. 366 367.

[21] *A Methodist Preacher*, op. cit., p. 58.

[22] *The Works of John Wesley*, Vol. XI, p. 366.

[23] *The Works of John Wesley*, Vol. I, p. 99.

[24] Ibid., Vol. XI, p. 367.

[25] W. H. Fitchett, op. cit., pp. 71, 72.

[26] A Methodist Preacher, op. cit., pp. 64f.

[27] A Methodist Preacher, op. cit, p. 68.

[28] Ibid.,p. 69.

29 A Methodist Preacher, op. cit, pp. 68f.

30 W. H. Fitchett, op. cit., p. 74; *The Works of John Wesley*, Vol. VIII, p. 348.

31 A Methodist Preacher, op. cit., p. 70.

32 Ibid., p.70.

33 *The Works of John Wesley*, Vol. III, p. 213.

34 A Methodist Preacher, op. cit., p. 73.

35 A Methodist Preacher, op. cit., 80.

36 *The Works of John Wesley*, Vol. I, p.23.

37 Ibid., Vol. XIII, p. 306.

38 *The Works of John Wesley*, Vol. I, pp. 75 77.

39 Ibid., Vol. I, p. 89.

40 Ibid., Vol. I, p. 86.

41 *The Works of John Wesley* Vol. I, p. 103.

42 A Methodist Preacher, op. cit., p. 106.

43 *The Works of John Wesley*, Vol. I, p. 93.

44 R. H. Fitchett, op. cit., p. 120.

45 The *Works of John Wesley*, Vol. I, pp. 96f.

46 Ibid., Vol. XIII, p. 307.

47 *The Works of John Wesley*, Vol. I, pp. 92 93.

48 *The Works of John Wesley*, Vol. VIII, pp. 252f.; XIII, p. 259; A Methodist Preacher, op. cit., pp. 123f.

49 *The Works of John Wesley*, Vol. VIII, pp. 269 271; A Methodist Preacher, op. cit., pp. 125f.

50 *The Works of John Wesley*, Vol. VIII, pp. 256f.

51 A Methodist Preacher, op. cit., pp. 126.

52 *The Methodist Hymn Book*, (London: The Methodist Publishing House, 1933), p. 53.

53 *The Works of John Wesley*, Vol. VIII. 340.

54 *Ibid., Vol. XIII, p. 258.*

55 Ibid., Vol. VIII, pp. 348 349.

56 *The Works of John Wesley*, Vol. VIII, p. 350.

57 Ibid., Vol. VIII, p. 341.

58 Ibid.,Vol. VIII, p. 344.

59 *The Works of John Wesley*, Vol. VIII, p. 346.

60 Ibid., Vol. VIII, p. 352.

61 *The Works of John Wesley*, Vol. VIII, p. 474.

62 *The Works of John Wesley*, Vol. VIII, p. 474.

63 *The Methodist Hymn Book*, pp. 48f.

64 *The Works of John Wesley*, Vol. X, p. 202.

65 Ibid., Vol. X. pp. 202f.

66 *The Works of John Wesley*, Vol. X, p. 203.

[67] *The Works of John Wesley*, Vol. X, p. 203.

[68] Henry Chadwick, *The Early Church History*,(Harmondsworth, Middlesex, England: Pengiun Books Ltd.,Reprinted 1974) P. 82.

[69] *The Works of John Wesley*, Vol. X, p. 366.

[70] *The Works of John Wesley*, Vol. X, pp. 366f.

[71] *The Works of John Wesley*, Vol. X, p. 367.

[72] Ibid.,Vol. X, pp. 367f.

[73] *The Works of John Wesley*, Vol. V, p. 311.

[74] Ibid., Vol. V, p. 311f.

[75] *The Works of John Wesley*, Vol. V, pp. 313f.

[76] Ibid., Vol. VII, p. 314.

[77] *John and Charles Wesley: Selected Prayers, Hymns, Journal Notes, Sermons Letters and Treatises*, Ed. Richard J. Payne, John Farina, etc. (New York, Ramsey, Toronto: Paulist Press, 1981), p.176.

[78]*John and Charles Wesley: Selected Prayers, Hymns, Journal Notes, Sermons Letters and Treatises*, Ed. Richard J. Payne, John Farina, etc., pp. 232f.

[79] *John and Charles Wesley: Selected Prayers, Hymns, Journal Notes, Sermons Letters and Treatises*, Ed. Richard J. Payne, John Farina, etc., p. 212.

[80] J. C. Ryle, *Holiness Its Nature, Hindrances, Difficulties, and Roots*, (Durham, England: Evangelical Press, 7th Impression, 1993), p. xvii.

[81] J. C. Ryle, *Holiness Its Nature, Hindrances, Difficulties, and Roots*, p. 39.

[82]Ibid., p. 45.

[83] Jerry Bridges, *The Pursuit of Holiness*, (Colorado: Navpress, 3rd printing, 1993), pp. 37 38.

Bibliography

A) Primary Sources

The Holy Bible, King James Version. Goedonville, Tennessee: Dugan Publishers, Inc., 1984

The Holy Bible, Revised Standard Version. London,Edinburgh,Paris,Melbourne, Johannesburg,Toronto,and New York: Thomas Nelson and Sons Ltd.,12th Impression, 1962.

The Thompson Chain-Reference Bible, New International Version. Grand Rapids, Michigan: Zondervan Bible Publishers, Second Printing, 1983.

The New English Bible with the Apocrypha. New York: Oxford University Press, 1971.

The Way, The Living Bible Illustrated. Wheaton, Illinois: Tyndale House Publishers, Sixth Printing, 1973.

God's Word, Today's Bible translation that says what it means. Grand Rapids, Michigan: World Publishing Ins., 1995.

B) Secondary Sources

Barclay, William. *The Letters to Philippians Colossians, Thessalonians*. Edinburgh: The Saint Andre Press, Third Impression, 1963.

Bridges, Jery. *The Pursuit of Holiness*. Colorado: Navpress, 3rd Printing, 1993.

Carpenter, Eugene & McCown, Wayne. (Eds) *Asbury Bible Commentary*. Grand Rapids, Michigan: Zondervan Publishing House, 1992.

Chadwick, Henry. *The Early Church*. Harmondsworth, England: Penguin Books Ltd., Reprinted 1974.

Church, Lesleie F. *The NIV Matthew Henry Commentary in One Volume*. Grand Rapids, Michigan: Zondervan Publishing House,1984.

Fitchett, W. H. *Wesley and His Century: A Study in Spiritual Forces*. Toronto:The Ryerson Press, 1920.

The Interpreter's Bible. New York, Nashville: Abingdon -Cokesbury Press, 1952, Vol. 12.

Jackman, Edward. Toronto: Celtic Ars of Canada, 1990.

Johnson, Paul. *A History of the Modern World from 1917 to the 1990s.* London: Weidenfeld and Nicolson, Revised Edition, 1983.

A Methodist Preacher, *John Wesley the Methodist: A Plain Account of His life and Work.* New York: Eaton & Mains, 1903.

The Methodist Hymn Book with Office. London : The Methodist Publishing House, 1933.

Osbeck, Kenneth W. *101 Hymn Stories.* Grand Rapids, Michigan: Kregal Publications, 1982.

Richardson, Cyril C. Ed. *Early Christian Fathers.* Philadelphia: The Westminster Press, Vol. I, n. D.

Ryle,R.C.HolinessIts Nature,Hindrances,Difficulties, and Roots.Durham, England: Eveangelical Press, 7th Impression, 1993.

Sproul, R. C. *The Holiness of God.* Wheaton,Illinois: Tyndale House Publishers, Inc., 1985.

Tozer, A. W. The Knowledge of the Holy. India: Alliance Publication, 1961

The Wesleyan Bible Commentary. Peabody, Massachusetts: Hendrickson Publishers. Reprinted 1986. Vol.6

Wesley, John. *The Works of John Wesley.* Grand Rapids, Michigan: Baker Book House, 3rd ed. 1984. Vol. 14.

-------------.*Explanatory Notes Upon the New Testament.* Grand Rapids, Michigan: Baker Book House, 1986. Vol.2

Wesley, John and Charles. *Selected Prayers, Hymns, Jpurnal Notes, Sermons Letters and Treatises.* eds. Richard J. Payne, John Forina, etc. New York, Ramsey, Toronto: Paulist Press, 1981.

Wuerl, Donald W. *Fathers of the Church.* Huntington, Indiana: Our Sunday Visitor, Inc.,2nd Printing 1977.

C) Other Sources

Neill, S., Goodwin, J., and Dowle, A., ed. *Concise Dictionary of the Bible.* London: United Society for Christian Literature, Lutterworth Press, 1966. Vol. 2.

The New American Encyclopedia. Philadelphia: The Publisher Agency Inc., 1974. Vol. 20.

Tan, Paul Lee. *Encyclopedia of 7700 Illustrations: Signs of the Times.* Rockville,Maryland: Assurance Publishers, 9th Printing, 1985.

Appendix-1

Rt. Rev. Dr. Daniel D. Rupwate has written more than three hundred textual sermons. Some of his textual sermons are published in the books, having different titles, mentioned below. This index booklet includes only fifteen books. Other sermons were privately published; they are excluded from the list. The index will help readers know where his textual sermons be found.

Name of the Book Book	Number
In Remembrance of the Life- Blood of Jesus Christ: Thirty-Six Textual Sermons on the Holy Communion	1
A Meditation on Good Friday: Textual Sermons on Seven Utterances of Jesus Christ from the Cross	2
The Good News of the Bible: Twenty-Five Textual Sermons on the Gospel of and About Jesus Christ Vol. I	3
The Good News of the Bible: Twenty-Five Textual Sermons on the Gospel of and About Jesus Christ Vol. II	4
Proven Divinity of Jesus Christ Through His Spiritual Titles and Exclusive claims	5
A Biblical Perspective on Mothers' Day, Fathers' Day and Children's Day	6
Biblical Foundations of Scripturally Based Spiritual Revival in the Church: Twenty-Eight Textual Sermons on Revivals and Reforms	7

The Teaching of Jesus Christ Through His Parables	8
A Biblical Administration of the Church and Society: Nineteen Textual Sermons on Administration of the Church And Fifteen Textual Sermons on Administration of Society	9
A Biblical leadership and the Church Discipline: Sixteen textual Sermons on the Biblical Leadership And the Church Discipline	10
The Call of God in Jesus Christ for Holiness and Social Morality: Fifteen Textual Sermons on Lent with Methodist Piety And Social Morality Or Scriptural Holiness of Methodism	11
Sanctified, Sacred, and Saved Life of Christians: Twenty-Nine Textual Sermons on Baptism, Marriage, and Funeral Services	12
Jesus of Nazareth, the Messiah or Christ: Thirty-One Textual Sermons on Proving Jesus as the Messiah or Christ.... (16 Textual Sermons on Christmas, 7 Textual Sermons on the Palm Sunday, 8 Textual Sermons on the Easter Sunday)	13
Covenantal Relationship Between the LORD God and His People: Nine Textual Sermons on Covenant Sunday or New Year Sunday with The Covenant Theology of the Rev. John Wesley and 'An Enlarged Historical Preface the Covenant with God Service	14
Thanking the LORD God on Two Special Occasions: Eleven Textual Sermons of the Thanksgiving Day and Two Textual Sermons on Church Anniversary Day	15
Covenantal Relationship between the Lord God and His People: Nine Textual Sermons on Covenant Sunday or New Year Sunday with 'The Covenant Theology of the Reverend John Wesley' and an Enlarged Historical Preface to the "Covenant with God Service."	16

Text	Book No.	Chapter No.
Genesis 2:18		
12	8	
4:9	9	20
22:16-18	14	1
24:50-51	12	9
Exodus		
4:13	9	1
14:15-16	9	2
20:12	6	7
Leviticus		
23:23-24	14	2
13:30	7	1
13:30	15	12
Deuteronomy		
5:15	7	2
8:10	15	1
8:14	7	3
16:14	14	3
32:6	15	2
Joshua		
23:14	12	15
I Samuel		
2:20	6	1

12:24-25	10	2
I Kings		
19:12	4	2
19:12	10	3
II Kings		
4:10	6	2
II Kings		
12:15	9	20
17:15	7	4
20:5-6	7	5
23:3	7	6
23:3	14	4
23:3	10	4
I Chronicles		
29:17	15	3
II Chronicles		
32:7-8	7	7
34:31	14	5
Nehemiah		
9:28	11	1
Psalms		
24:3-4	11	2
26:1	10	5
50:23	15	4

51:10	11	3
73:25	12	16
82:3-4	9	21
103:2-5	15	5

Psalms

111:10	10	6
112:5-6	12	17
116:15	12	18
119:9	6	13
121:1-2	11	4
127:1	12	10

Proverbs

2:12	6	14
3:27	9	22
9:10	7	8
10:1	6	15
10:7	12	19
11:24	15	6
13:21	9	23
19:18	6	16
20:7	6	8
22:6	6	17
23:13-14	6	9
24:3	7	9

25:4-5	9	24
29:15	6	3
29:15	6	18
29:18	9	25
31:20	6	4
31:30	6	5

Ecclesiastes

12:13-14	10	7

Isaiah

4:4	11	5
11:1	7	10
11:1	9	3
25:8	12	20
28:26	9	26
32:17	9	27
6:3	12	21

Jeremiah

5:30-31	10	8
18:4	11	6

Ezekiel

11:19-20	14	6
34:4	9	28

Hosea

6:1-2	12	22

Amos

3:7	9	4
5:24	9	29

Micah

5:2	13	1

Habakkuk

3:17-18	15	7

Haggai

1:9-10	9	5
2:9	15	8

Zechariah

4:6	7	1

Matthew

1:1	5	1
1:21	13	2
1:23	13	3
2:3	13	4
2:10-11	13	5
2:12	13	6
3:11	12	1
5:13	8	2

Matthew

5:14-15	8	3

5:17	4	3
5:20	9	6
7:14	8	3
7:18-19	8	5
7:25	8	6
7:28-29	3	2
8:8	7	12
8:17	3	3
9:17	8	7
10:32-33	4	4
12:45	8	8
13:8	8	9
13:9	3	4
13:30	8	10
13:32	8	11
13:44	8	12
13:45-46	8	13
13:47	8	14
13:52	8	15
16:16	5	2
16:23	4	5
18:35	8	16
19:14	12	2
20:16	8	17

20:31	8	18
21:8	13	17
21:9	13	18

Matthew

21:13	10	9
21:16	13	19
21:41	8	19
21:42	3	5
22:12	8	20
25:13	8	21
25:40	9	30
25:45	9	31
25:45-46	8	22
26:27	1	1
26:29	1	2
26:38	11	7
26:64	5	3
26:66	11	8
27:46	2	4

Mark

1:14-15	4	6
1:22	3	6
4:26-29	8	23
8:35	4	7

10:30	4	8
11:9-10	13	20
16:3	13	24

Luke

2:7	13	7
2:10	13	8
2:11	13	9
2:21	13	10
2:34-35	13	11

Luke

2:52	6	19
2:21	12	3
4:18-19	3	7
5:4-5	7	13
7:32	8	24
7:47	8	25
9:62	4	9
10:36-37	8	26
11:9	8	27
12:21	8	28
12:48	8	29
13:5	11	9
13:8-9	8	30
13:21	8	31

13:24	8	32
14:11	8	33
14:28	8	34
15:7	8	35
15:10	8	36
15:32	8	37
16:10	8	38
16:15	10	10
16:25	8	39
17:18	15	9
18:7-8	8	40
18:14	8	41
19:26	8	42
21:3	15	10
22:13	1	3

Luke

22:15	1	4
22:20	1	5
23:24	2	1
23:42-43	2	2
23:46	2	7
24:5	13	25
24:30-31	1	6
24:46-47	3	8

John

1:14	5	4
1:14	13	12
2:17	13	21
3:3	7	14
3:16	3	9
3:30	13	13
4:13-14	5	7
4:21	11	10
4:26	5	5
4:42	9	7
6:35	5	8
6:35	1	7
6:53	1	8
8:12	5	9
8:31-32	7	15
8:42	6	10
8:58	5	10
10:7	5	11
10:11	10	11
10:11	5	12

John

11:25	5	13
12:5	9	32

12:9	13	22
12:14-15	13	23
12:35-36	12	23
13:13	5	6
13:15	9	8
13:18	1	9
14:6	5	14
15:4	7	16
15:10	6	11
15:13-14	1	10
19:26-27	2	3
19:28	2	5
19:30	2	6
21:12	1	11
21:15	13	26
21:18-19	13	27

Acts

6:3	9	9
19:5-6	12	4
20:24	4	10
20:28	1	12

Romans

1:16-17	3	10
2:29	14	7

3:25	1	13
5:8	3	11
5:9	1	14

Romans

5:18	3	12
6:4	12	5
8:18	12	24
10:15	4	11
12:2	7	17
12:9	10	12
13:12-13	4	12
15:18	10	13
16:18	10	14

I Corinthians

10:16	1	17
10:21	1	18
10:33-11:1	7	19
11:26	1	19
11:29	1	20
13:5	12	11
15:17	13	28

II Corinthians

2:15-16	3	15
3:9	3	16

4:3-4	3	17
4:6	3	18
4:18	12	25
5:15	1	21
5:17	14	8
5:20-21	3	19
7:10	11	12
9:8	15	11
Galatians		
1:9	4	16
1:11-12	3	20
2:20	4	17
2:20	7	20
3:13	3	21
4:4-5	4	18
5:1	4	19
Ephesians		
1:13-14	4	20
2:13	1	22
2:15-16	3	22
3:6	3	23
3:17-18	13	14
4:3	9	33
4:5	12	6

I Timothy		
6:11	15	13
II Timothy		
1:5	6	6
1:10	4	24
2:21	11	14
3:5	7	21
3:15	6	20
4:21	9	18
Titus		
2:11-12	7	22
2:11-12	11	15
Hebrews		
2:11	13	16
2:14	1	25
4:9-10	12	26
8:6	1	26
9:14	1	27
9:22	1	28
10:19-20	1	29
11:9-1	12	27
Hebrews		
12:5-6	6	12

13:4	12	13
13:12	1	30

James

2:13	7	24
3:17 7 25		

I Peter

1:2	1	31
1:12	4	25
1:17	10	17
1:18-19	1	32
2:24-25	3	26
3:21	12	7
4:17	4	26

II Peter

1:5-7	4	27
1:8	4	28

I John

1:7	1	33
2:29	7	26
3:14	7	27
5:5	13	31

III John

4	12	14

Appendix-II
The Prophets and the Kings in the Old Testament

Before the kingdom of Israel was established, the LORD God chose priest Samuel to look after the spiritual welfare of the people of Israel. God asked Samuel to anoint Saul as the first king of the Israel. (I Sam. 10: 1) The priest Samuel was also anointed as a prophet of the people of Israel. It means that prophethood originated with Samuel. King Saul failed to carry out a command of the LORD God, therefore God asked prophet Samuel to anoint David as the successor of King Saul (I Sam. 16:13). After King David, his son Solomon became the king of the Israel. After Solomon, his son Rehoboam became the king. During his period, the kingdom of Israel was divided. The southern kingdom was called the kingdom of Judah and the norther kingdom was called the kingdom of Israel. There kingdoms were destroyed by the foreign powers and Jews were taken into captivity. They settled in many parts of the world. The Interpreters' Bible (volume I, pp. 145-148) has given a chart, detailing the names of the kingdoms of Judah and Israel and their dates of reigning. The chart also mentions the events after the destruction of those kingdoms. The chart, however, did not mention the names of the prophets against the names of the kings. It would useful to include the names of the prophets which would suggest their possible dates, along with the kings and the historical events. The writer of the article is attempting to present a wider chart in order to include the prophets.

Prophet	King	
Samuel	Saul (1044-1004 B. C.)	
	David (1002-962 B. C.)	
Nathan (II Sam. 7:2)		
Gad (II Sam. 24:11)		
Nathan (I Kg. 1:32-34) Solomon (962-922 B. C.)		

	King of Judah	King of Israel
	Rehoboam (922-915 B. C.)	Jeroboam (922-901)
	Abijam (915-913 B. C	Nadab (901-900 B. C.)
	Asa (913-873 B. C.)	Baasha (900-877 B. C.)
		Elah (877-876 B. C.) Zimri (876) 7 days
	Jehoshaphat (837-849 B. C.)	Omri (876-869 B. C.)
Elijah (I Kg. 18:2)		Ahab (869-850 B. C.)
Elisha (I Kg. 19:16)		

	King of Judah	King of Israel Ahaziah (850-849 B. C.)
	Jehoram (849-842 B. C.)	Joram (849-842 B. C.)
	Ahaziah (842 B. C.)	
	Athaliah (842-837 B. C.) (Queen)	Jehu (842-815)
	Jehoash (837-800 B. C.)	Joahaz (815-801 B. C.)
	Amaziah (800-783 B. C.)	Joash (801-786 B. C.)
Isaiah (1:1)	Uzziah (Azariah) 783-742 B. C.)	Jeroboam (786-746 B. C.)
Amos (1:1)		

Micah (1:1)   Jotham (750-742 B. C.) regent

Hosea (1:1)   Ahaz (735-715 (B. C.)   Jeroboam (786-746 B. C.)

Zechariah (746-745 B. C.) months

Shallum (745 B. C.) 1 month

Jotham (742-735 B. C.), king Menahem (745-738 B. C.)

Ahaz (735-715 B. C.)   Pekahia (738-737 B. C.)

Pekah (737-732 B. C.)

Hoshea (732-724 B. C.)

Tiglath-pileser III of Assyria enthroned Hoshea in 732 B. C.

King of Judah

Hezekiah (715-687 B. C.)

Habakkuk   Manasseh (687-642 B. C.)

Amon (642-640 B. C.)

Jeremiah (1:2)   Josiah (640-609 B. C.)

Zephaniah (1:1) Jehoahaz 609 B. C.)

3 months

Daniel (1:1)   Jehoiakim (609-598 B. C.) King Nebuchadnezer of Babylon (605-562 B. C.) besieged Jerusalem and King Jehoiakim was taken into captivity

Ezekiel (1:2)   Jehoiachin (598 B. C.)

3 months

Zedekiah (598-587 B. C.)   Jerusalem destroyed,

Jeremiah (52:30)   Deportation of Jews

Persian King

Cyrus (539-530 B. C.)   Edit for return of the Jews
                         Zerubbabel, governor of
                         Judah

Haggai (1:1)   (538-446 B.C.)

Darius I (522-486 B. C.)   Work on the temple
                            (520-516 B. C.)

Artaxerexes I (465-424 B. C.)   Return of Ezra (548 B. C.)

Nehemiah, governor of Judah (445-433 B. C.)

Zechariah
(1:1, 7; 7:1)   King Darius I (522-486 B. C.)

Artaxeres II (404-358 B. C.)   Return of Ezra (397 B. C.)

Other Publications

Books

Thanking the Lord God on Two Special Occasions: Eleven Textual Sermons on Thanksgiving Day and Two Textual Sermons on Church Anniversary Day" Delhi. India: ISPCK, 2019.

Jesus of Nazareth, the Messiah or Christ: Thirty-one Textual Sermons on Proving Jesus of Nazareth as Messiah or Christ, with an Essay, 'A Theological Significance of Forty Days' Delhi. India: ISPCK, 2018.

A Biblical Administration of the Church and Society: Nineteen Textual Sermons on Administration of the Church and Fifteen Textual Sermons on Administration of Society, Delhi, India: ISPCK, 2016.

The Teaching of Jesus Christ Through His Parables: Forty-one Textual Sermons on the Parables of Jesus Christ, Delhi, India: ISPCK, 2016.

Biblical Foundations of Scripturally Based Spiritual Revivals in the Church: Twenty Eight Textual Sermons on revivals and Reform and Rev. John Wesley's Theology of 'the New Birth', ISPCK, 2015.

A Biblical Perspective on Mothers' Day, Fathers' Day, and Children's Day, Delhi, India, ISPCK, 2014.

The Good News of the Bible: Twenty Five Textual Sermons on the Gospel of and About Jesus Christ, Vol. I, Delhi, India, ISPCK, 2014.

The Good News of the Bible: Twenty Seven Textual Sermons on the Gospel of and About Jesus Christ, Vol. II, Delhi, India, ISPCK, a2014.

Proven Divinity of Jesus Christ Through His Scriptural Titles and Exceptional Claims, Delhi, India, ISPCK. 2014.

In Remembrance of the Life-Blood of Jesus Christ: Thirty-Six Textual Sermons on the Holy Communion, Pune India, The Word of Life Publication, 2003.

Negro Methodist Churches, Rev. John Wesley's Thoughts Upon Slavery, and His Struggle Against Slavery, 1998

The Book of Offices for the British Methodist Episcopal Church, 1998.

A Worship Manual for a Scriptural or Methodist Order of Service, 2005.

Biblical Solutions to the Problems of a Church: Fifteen Textual Sermons, delivered at Annual and General Conferences of the B. M. E. Church of Canada, 1998.

A Scriptural Vindication of the Articles of Religion: Twenty-five Articles of Religion of Methodism with The Reverend John Wesley's Acts of and Thoughts about Baptism, 2010.

A Selective Commentary on a Comparative Study of the Bible and the Koran, Wilmington, IN, U. S. A.: Xlibris, 2020.

Covenantal Relationship Between the Lord God and His People: Nine Textual Sermons on Covenant Sunday or New Year Sunday with 'The Covenant Theology of the Reverend John Wesley' and "An Enlarged Historical Preface to 'Covenant Service with God Service', Delhi: India: ISPCK, 2019.

Booklets

A Meditation on Good Friday: Textual Sermons on Seven Utterances of Jesus Christ from the Cross, Pune, India: Sumitra Prakashan, 2012.

A Historical Significance of the "salem Chapel" with reference to the Underground Railroad Movement and a tribute to Harriet Tubman, Second or Revised edition, 2016.

Christianity in the Context of the Indian Way of Life (a book on social, religious, and political issues, in Marathi), Bangalore,

India: Christian Institute for the Study of Region & Society, 1979.

Socio-Religious Policies of the British Methodist Episcopal Church of Canada, Toronto: B. M. E. Church Conference, 1990.

A Historical Significance of "Salem Chapel" with Reference to Underground Railroad Movement, 2006.

Essays

'The Bible and Racism', "Mukti", Bimonthly, Vol. 1, no. 4 and 5, Toronto, 1982, 1983.

Christian Participation in Politics', "Apostle", The B. M. E. Church of Canada Publication, May 1979.

The Covenant Theology of John Wesley, Toronto: Canadian Methodist Historical Society, 1993.

Methodist Piety and Social Morality or Scriptural Holiness of Methodism (Toronto: Canadian Methodist Historical Society, 1995).

A Versatile Significance of Rta, (Poona, India: Bhandarkar Oriental Research Institute, 1982).

'A Theological Significance of Forty Days,' Jesus of Nazareth, The Messiah or Christ: Thirty-two Textual Sermons on Providing Jesus of Nazareth as Messiah or Christ, with an Essay, 'Theological Significane of Forty Days,' ISPCK, 2018, pp. 345-351.

A Word about the Author and the Book

The Rt. Rev. Dr. Daniel D. Rupwate, B. A. (Hons.), B. D., M. Th., Ph. D., was the General Superintendent of the British Methodist Episcopal Church of Canada from 1987 to 1998. He was born in Maharashtra (Bombay) State in India. He was graduated from the University Pune (Poona) in 1963 with B. A. (Hons.). As far as his training in a theology is concerned, he obtained B. D. in 1967 and M. Th. in 1970, from Senate of Serampore. Whilst in India, he served the Methodist Church in Southern Asia as a Minister in Nagpur, Pune, and Mumbai. He was a lecturer in the United Theological College, Pune, for a year. He served as a Regional Secretary of Maharashtra State of the Christian Institute for the Study of Religion & Society. Some of his essays were published in a newspaper and were later compiled in a booklet in Marathi and published in 1974. The English subtitle for this booklet is "Christianity in the Context of the Indian Way of Life." In 1980 he obtained Ph. D. from McMaster University, Hamilton, Canada. He joined the ministry of the British Methodist Episcopal Church of Canada in 1978 and served as a Minister in Toronto, East York, Brantford, St. Catharines, and Niagara Falls, Ontario. He also served as the General Secretary of the B. M. E. Church Conference from 1982 to 1986. He wrote a few essays for Canadian Methodist Historical Society, which were published by the said organization.

He continues to do research and writing on Methodism. He wrote a book "Negro Methodist Churches, Rev. John Wesley's Thoughts Upon Slavery, and His Struggle Against Slavery" in 1998, which may help readers know the significant contributions of the Rev. John Wesley, a founder of Methodism, towards propagating the gospel and combatting racism in the world.

He delivered textual sermons at the Annual and General Conference of the B. M. E. Church. He published the book, "Biblical Solutions to Problems of a Church: Fifteen Textual Sermons of the General Superintendent, Delivered at Annual and General Conferences" in 1998.

He took a major responsibility to publish "Book of Offices for the British Methodist Episcopal Church" in 1998. This book is his valuable contribution to the said church.

He prepared a worship manual for a Scriptural or Methodist Order of Service and published this book in 2005.

His other publications are given at the end of the book. They are his textual sermons, published under different titles. Those sermons comprehensively deal with almost every aspect of Christian life and the biblical theology.

His book, " THE CALL OF GOD IN JESUS CHRIST FOR HOLINESS AND SOCIAL MORALITY

FIFTEEN TEXTUAL SERMONS ON THE LENT WITH 'METHODIST PIETY AND SOCIAL MORALITY OR SCRIPTURAL HOLINESS OF METHODISM' is to explain the biblical concept of holiness and to ask believers in Jesus Christ to practice it in their individual and social [DR1] [DR1]life so that they demonstrate their call for holiness and justice. Methodism is a biblical Christianity; its founders, John Wesley and Charles Wesley, were raised in pietistic family background. They confirmed and lived life of holiness and justice. They taught the biblical holiness to their followers. This book will help know how the biblical holiness is different from the concepts of holiness of other creeds or religions.

Rev. Dr. Jasmin Hivale-Quibell, B. A. (Hons.), M. R. E., M. Div., D. Th., A Clergy in Anglican Church, Niagara-on the Lake, Ontario, Canada.

www.ingramcontent.com/pod-product-compliance
Lightning Source LLC
Chambersburg PA
CBHW061433150726
47987CB00001B/196